Y0-BFD-366

The Virtue of Fly Fishing

By Mark Bachmann

Acknowledgements

I suppose everyone who touches your life in some way influences each of your accomplishments and with or without intent, alters the navigation of your life's journey. If that is true, then the ones with the vilest of evil intentions and no regard for your welfare at all may have a positive effect by strengthening your resolve to succeed and triumph over evil. But naming all of that kind would make the list of helpers much too complicated to comprehend. Because of that, I will leave out most evil personalities except Adolf Hitler (never a fan) who must have influenced my mother and father with the need to hold on tighter to each other on the night I was conceived just shortly before dad went to Europe. So, thanks Adolf for bolstering the American testosterone levels and thanks dad for making the thrust that gave me the speed to win the race, and thanks mom for enjoying the process that got me started.

Even though my parents wanted a boy to carry on the family name, I was a puzzle they never quite solved. I was supposed to be an agrarian scholar like my father wanted to be. He was exceedingly bright and practical at surviving with dignity and was very well read on many worthwhile subjects. My father only had seven years of formal education. All the few people who really knew him would have described him as a well-educated man. His son, however, had twelve years of education and at seventeen knew everything about everything but had little interest in agriculture or anything practical.

Little Mark was born with a reading disability. From the first through the third grades the English language was beyond my grasp. Mom and Dad subscribed to the best magazines; National Geographic, Scientific American, Mechanics Illustrated, Family Circle, and Readers Digest were regularly read to us kids at an early age to instill reading curiosity in me and my two sisters. My mother thought that comic books were a total waste of time and banned them from our house. We children read scientifically factual material rather than degenerate fantasy comic books. My school buddies all had comic books. I started investigating comic books to see why mom objected to them, and in doing so I taught myself to read by comparing the words to the pictures. By the end of the fourth grade my reading skills surpassed the last three elementary grades. According to my eighth grade SAT test scores, I was reading with the speed, comprehension, and retention comparable to a senior in college. I entered high school as a skillful and avid reader. I read the subscription magazines and library books from cover to cover. My parents had kindled the thirst for knowledge, but spelling and sentence structure eluded me.

My freshman home room was my first high school English class taught by Ms. Hellen Curtis who taught by diagramming sentences to identify their parts. I never did get the practical application to the formula. My grades fell with the struggle, and I felt miserable. In the eleventh grade I took an elective creative writing class from a vibrant, out-going, teacher named Carol Rausch. She helped me find a style to sentence structure and was supportive enough to give me confidence that with more practice, I could succeed in telling stories on paper. However, my real break came from a bridge construction foreman with an eighth grade education named Walt Crownover. He explained to me his formula for figuring out problems, "Any damn fool can figure out "how" if he can figure out "why." Then after most of my children had studied under her, I hired primary school English teacher, Janine Boldt to tutor me in writing when I was past thirty. She helped clean up my story writing skills, and her effects were instantaneous. With that in mind, my wife Patty has been the focus of my success in all my varied projects by providing me with a harmonious environment in which to allow my creative juices to flow unimpeded without undue distractions. My friend Henry Carlile introduced me to Strunk and White's, *The Elements of Style,* and took the time to show me how to use it by editing and restructuring some of my recent stuff. My granddaughter, Billy Jean Bachmann gave me companionship and inspiration, then let me lean on her and get this project rolling. Charissa Jones-Lilly continually inspires my writing and straightens out my organization and story line by asking questions that draw out more details and fill in the gaps. Jim Highland encourages me to not worry about being politically correct and let my passion rise to the surface, then let the chips fall as they may. And most of all I'd like to thank all of the anglers and companions who have let me share their ideals and adventures which have added spice to my life and provided me with interesting situations to write about. Here's hoping you all *Fish long & prosper!*

Foreword. Why Fly Fish?

"What doesn't kill me makes me stronger

Friedrich Nietzsche, 1888.

Most anglers who choose fly fishing as a recreation don't consider it a sport that can kill you. I mean, fly fishing for steelhead with a two-hand fly rod isn't comparable to hunting lions with a rifle. Yet death is death, and it doesn't matter whether it is caused by slashing claws, fangs, or lungs full of water. I have personally known more men who have drowned while pursuing steelhead than were mauled by big cats. Both men I knew that eventually were overpowered by the currents of a big river were extreme risk-takers. Neither died while fishing with me, but I had cautioned both of them after they had showcased their wading skills while using my guide service. It was bound to happen sooner or later. And when it did eventually happen to each, the fly-fishing community bewailed the tragedies. But I thought, "What better way to meet your maker than in a place you love, doing something you love!" Thank goodness I had enough common sense, not to mention how I felt about the deaths, while in conversations with either widow.

What better way to live, than doing something you love to do? Taking that thought to the limits would seem to entail doing something you love, in a place you love, and sharing it with someone you love. So, I became a fly-fishing guide and

shop owner in partnership with my wife, Patty. But, quite frankly, if I am to meet my maker by drowning in a river I love, I hope she isn't there as a witness to the event, nor do I wish her to be a participant in this ending.

To some new fly fishers, simply casting the fly to a specific fish is beyond their skill level, even when casting at short distances from a boat guided by a competent professional. The fly-fishing industry knows this and capitalizes by telling people that they can buy a magic fly rod that will compensate for their lack of training, dedication, physical fitness, untrained eyesight, and overall lack of skills. The fly-fishing industry trains guides not to criticize clients, provide instructions, or catch fish in front of their clients. Undoubtedly, my tips went way up when I started following these rules. But the catch in my boat went way down as well. Sometimes I wonder if I sold out. But on the other hand, most would agree that it is the intelligent businessperson who cuts labor and increases profit. I still save my old self for students who don't mind being pushed and realize that you get out of anything in proportion to what you put into it. In the sport of fly fishing, if your goal is to catch fish, you must be fully engaged to meet your own expectations. If your goal is to catch larger-than-average fish from public water, you must evolve skills superior to your competition. In other words, the more difficult the water is to fish, the fewer anglers will fish it and the more rested the fish will be. This is undoubtedly the case when fishing for steelhead in Pacific Northwest Rivers.

When fishing unfamiliar water or for new fish species, I hire guides who have never read the "nice guy" manuals, or I instruct them I wasn't interested in being coddled or entertained. I wanted to learn from them, and they could dispense with being politically correct

if I wasn't getting their messages. Sometimes I would hand them my rod and fly collection and ask them to demonstrate how it was done. Invariably I was rewarded with some new insights. I was often amazed at how easily many of these guides caught fish I thought were difficult. But, of course, everything is easy if you know how to do it. An angler who can cast his fly ten feet back under the overhanging mangroves is more likely to catch snook than those who can't. An angler who can drop his crab two feet in front of a head-on permit at eighty feet with a perfectly straight line will stick every one of them. Just like an angler who can cast a large intruder a hundred feet with a Skagit head while wading a large, cold winter river wasn't born with the skills. That person likely got lessons from someone, has an obsessive personality, and has practiced for several seasons. That person already seeks out and knows The Virtue of Fly Fishing as an avenue to strengthen one's body, gain coordination, and focus one's senses. And if those are some of your goals, this book will give you valuable insights and provide entertainment as well.

Table of Contents

Chapter 1

The Virtue of Hard Water

"The only impossible journey is the one you never begin."
Tony Robbins

In September 1986, I was forty-two years old, my body hard and lean from years of manual labor. It was my fifth season as a professional fly-fishing guide in Oregon, and the Deschutes River was at its peak for summer steelhead. This was a couple of years before Columbia River Tribes were geared up to capitalize on the Judge Boldt Decision, which gave them rights to harvest half the steelhead and salmon in the Columbia River upstream from Bonneville Dam. It was also a time when use of the river by sport fishermen had decreased because of more restrictive harvest regulations. The use of bait had been prohibited on the Deschutes. Many anglers rebelled and stopped fishing there, believing that steelhead could only be caught with bait. Because I knew otherwise my business had boomed. It was prime time for steelhead, yet fewer anglers pursued them. It was also the interval between introduction of regulations to conserve wild fish and the Spey-rod revolution that would dawn after 1990 in the Pacific Northwest and make fly fishing for steelhead easier for many anglers. Before 1990 most steelhead anglers had fished with single-hand seven or eight-weight rods nine to ten feet in length. Oregon Fish and Wildlife regulations for the Deschutes stipulated boats could be used for transportation only. Anglers could not fish from them. It was a wade fishery and remains so to this day. But because much of the Deschutes bottom is comprised of large angular cobble and basalt ledges it is challenging to wade.

Brad, Al, and I were on a three-day float from Mack's Canyon to the mouth of the Deschutes where it joins the Columbia River, a twenty-five-mile trip. After floating about eight miles, we stopped at several spots to fish. During this time, Brad managed to hook two steelhead and land one. Al had also landed one, all in bright sunshine. This stretch of river was full of fish. It was lunchtime, so I set up camp, a large screen-house for cooking and dining where I slept at night. Brad and Al shared the second tent, a large dome with two portable folding cots. Inside the screen-house I set up folding tables, chairs, a propane two-burner stove, barbeque, and coolers we had brought downriver with us in my seventeen-foot aluminum drift boat. My habit in those days was to spend two nights in a camp, if there were decent numbers of steelhead in the camp water. Or I would break camp if there were no fish and move downriver several miles and set up a second camp. Our camp was in a protected alder grove on a wide flat, water perfect for fly fishing. The fish were there. We all agreed we would be unlikely to move camp the next day.

If we did move, it would be after the morning fishing session during the brightest part of the day when fishing was the least productive. Summer steelhead are usually most active during low-light conditions. This is especially true on the Deschutes River, which runs north, where every steelhead faces into the sun during most daylight hours. Like us, they have a hard time seeing directly into sunlight.

Now fading light from the setting sun illuminated only the top third of a shear, towering basalt cliff on the opposite shore of the broad river. This gigantic stone bulwark would keep the camp and camp water in shade until nearly noon tomorrow. Now the waning light was approaching magic-time when it is neither day nor dark, a brief period in the daily cycle of the sun when everything is possible. The shade from the lower canyon wall to the west made me rush through tall dry grass at the lowest level of the deep canyon, my destination the smooth ledge-studded tail out a quarter of a mile upstream from camp. I had left Brad and Al in the camp riffle, where they had been moving and hooking steelhead all afternoon. They didn't need my help or criticism.

Above camp, the river broke along a brush-covered bank so steep the railroad was nearly overhead. This was on the deeper outside curve of a sweeping bend, the wrong side of the river. Partway through the curve, a huge red alder leaned out over the water, its lower limbs nearly touching the surface. I had rowed by this place dozens of times before, surveying the river bottom from a moving drift boat. It was always deserted. To me, it looked like great holding water for steelhead but difficult to fish with a fly. It was certainly not a place to put clients until I had fished it myself to see if it was even possible. My confidence had never equaled my curiosity…until this afternoon.

A short way downstream from the alder I stopped and surveyed the river from a high vantage point on an old deer trail twenty feet above the water and decided the water above the alder looked too tough for the time I had left before dark. I would start just below the tree, but the huge splash of a Steelhead rolling upstream of the alder changed my mind. A fish you have located is always the best option.

A short hike upstream and descent of the steep grade brought me to the water's edge twenty feet upstream of the fish. A narrow-submerged ledge gave me footing three feet off the bank. I stripped ten feet of bright floating fly line from the reel and checked the leader and the hook point on my size four purple fly. Everything was perfect. A brisk roll cast shot the fly forty-five degrees downstream across the current. The line and leader landed straight. The fly came under tension as it entered the water. I let the fly lead the rod tip as the fly swung with a light touch and gentle action. It had moved two feet when a positive tug pulled line from the reel. I raised my hand to let the middle of the rod absorb the shock as the silver fish writhed to the surface and exerted its power against the screaming reel until he had reached mid-river in front of me. The fight was ferocious but over quickly. I tailed and revived the bright ten-pound hatchery buck and quickly released him.

Re-surveying the water in front of me I realized I had been so focused on the placement of that fish and the strike had come so quickly I hadn't taken the time to read the water. The water’s surface was slick but moving at a good speed that spanned the river. In places, underwater ledges broke the surface with flat seamy boils. The nearest ledge was sixty feet in front of me. The streamside brush nearly touched my back and was higher than my head. Leaning out from my purchase on the narrow ledge, I could expect no more than five feet of clearance for a back loop to form my roll cast. Darkness was fast approaching and didn't give me much time to deliberate. I started with the same cast that took the fish, then lengthened the line three feet for the next cast. The fly slid down the current and hung under the alder branches below me. I lengthened the line for a fourth cast. The next fish took just as I was starting to lift line for my upstream haul. It turned downstream jerking the rod tip a foot under water before erupting from the surface. The shock was too much for the ten-pound tippet. My purple Street Walker fly probably decorated that eight-pounder's jaw for most of the evening, and it left me in the vacuum that follows a peak surge of adrenaline.

The whole tippet was gone. The leader had parted at the blood knot. I fumbled for my tippet dispenser and unrolled three feet of hard Maxima, figuring that a short stiff tippet would turn over. The fish had taken my last Street Walker which I replaced with a size two low water Undertaker, a sleek dark pattern that had proven itself many times in fading light. I covered the same water in the same manner as before, but as I extended the casts, I had to make repeated small upstream mends to maintain proper fly speed and make it come across on a slow arc. The next strike came fifteen feet straight out beyond the alder, a gentle pluck. I was still pumped from my encounter with the previous fish, over-reacted, and the hook instantly came free.

Four casts later the fly was nearly to the wake caused by an underwater ledge when the line tightened, and I dropped the rod tip. After a perceptible pause the line came tight with a thunk. A beautiful six-pound wild hen was landed after a long intense battle I thought would leave all other resident fish in total shock.

As the twilight lingered, Brad waded through the edge of a shallow riffle above camp, his left-handed casting stroke barely discernible in the distance. *Should I invite him to join me and share the fun?* I wondered. He was too far away for the remaining light. A Night Hawk zig zagged across the river between us. Tonight, I would keep this steelhead Eden for myself and bring him here in the morning. Pungent aromas from the sage-covered canyon and the river's earthy damp margins filled the evening as I once more surveyed my private piscatorial oasis.

Intermittent turbulence betrayed a possible jog in the side of the far-off ledge that still faced me; a perfect cove for steelhead to shelter in, but a long cast almost straight across from me with no chance to swing the fly through it. I would have to cast to the top of the cove and then make a long reach mend to hold the fly in the sweet spot for as long as possible. It took several frustrating tries before the fly settled into a seam of calm water between two sets of turbulence. The strike was vicious as a big Steelhead boiled the surface, took my fly, and sped downstream. After a long, dogged fight. the buck came to hand in the dark.

Brad flipped the switch on the self-starting lantern as I approached the cook tent. Al peered over his finely sculptured meerschaum pipe and purred, “How’d you do, boss?"

“Boys, have I got a place to show you in the morning! It’s hard water to fish, but it is full of steelhead.”

The chapter you have just read is a window into the past. It all happened in eleven hours in late September of 1986. The number of fish caught in the amount of time was not unusual for that month in that year, nor was it the top day. Nineteen eighty-six was the all-time best year for catch numbers in my forty plus years of guiding steelhead fly fishing trips. We had the least amount of competition from other anglers or commercial fishermen and an adequate run size of steelhead. In 1986 379,891 steelhead passed Bonneville Dam on the Columbia River. It was the largest run recorded up to that time. My clientele was mature but young enough to be strong and agile, and many had the skills needed and the inclination to make their pet guide look good. In 2001 the fish run record was broken with 633,073, my second. best year. The last good year was 2014 with 325,965. Since then, the runs have been in decline. I fret like everyone does, then remind myself I don't fish for steelhead because it's easy. I do it because it is big boy stuff but I have to be reminded that I am a big boy and should act like one. Even during the glory years there were fishless days. Fly fishing for steelhead is not a casual sport.

This story was written in 1990 after I took a short refresher writing class. English was my worst subject in school. The easiest stories to write are about times of discovery. That is why I fish, for those times when new discoveries are made. Those times clear the cobwebs from human brains. Real adventures only happen when new things are being tried; a new place, a new friend, a new technique, a new threshold, or a new risk is overcome. The best place to have adventures is in the outdoors because mother nature has no bias if you are playing against yourself.

Chapter 2

A Spark in the Gloom

The future belongs to those who believe in the beauty of their dreams.
- Eleanor Roosevelt

Against all odds, a woman wrote the first book to mention fly fishing in English in the early 1400s. At that time, the concept of a 'glass ceiling' did not exist as it does today. Women during the early Renaissance had extremely limited access to education or the tools needed to record information. In 1400, most people in Europe were illiterate. Few kings could read or write. Universal educational systems weren't developed in any country. Before the printing press, books were rare and very expensive in that era. Officers of the male-dominated Church monopolized literacy. Their focus was the Bible, written only in Latin. It had to be hand-copied in select monasteries, one page at a time. Women were routinely excluded from this process.

After the Romans left in 410 A.D., England experienced a thousand years of continuous internal warfare. As a result, there hadn't been much progress in England. There were few paved roads. Most people were born, lived, and died within a ten-mile radius. People's worldview was very limited.

The prevailing belief was that the Earth was flat and the center of the Cosmos, and our sun revolved around it. They also believed that God created human life, Adam and Eve. He placed them in the beautiful garden of Eden. However, Eve succumbed to the temptations of Satan when she ate the forbidden fruit of knowledge. They were cast out of Eden to roam the Earth, where God granted them dominion.

For millennia, it was the belief that upon death believers go to Heaven and experience eternal bliss. Non-believers are rejected by God and received by Satan, where they fuel the fires of Hell for eternity. Until recently, the belief has been that the only path to Heaven is through the church. If anyone disbelieved and or disobeyed, they risked being publicly burned at the stake as an example of Hell's reality, a powerful deterrent against curiosity. The promoted vision was one of total war between God and Satan, with the salvation of human souls as the offered prize.

In 1400 A.D., few thought about their effects on the natural environment. Fate and destiny were at the discretion of Divine Will. Previously in 1347, Satan had unleashed the ghastly Black Death Plague, cutting Europe's human population in half. Personal hygiene was not regularly practiced, and medical treatments as we know them were not available. Even livestock were infected. For the majority of people, their lives were filled with fear, filth, and death. There were no options besides staying on your knees and praying you didn't go to Hell covered with the black, pus oozing pox and suffering for eternity.

Within the conservatism of the Catholic Christian power structure in the early 1400s, a tiny spark was lit in the most repressed entity of the Church. In a convent, an English noblewoman, Dame Julianna Berners, made a small entry into the book of St. Albans called "A Treatise of Fishing with an Angel." It is estimated to have been written around 1421 in Old English (not Latin). The word for Angel was pronounced with a hard "g" like angle, the basis for the word's angler & angling. "The Treatise" contained instructions on building rods and lines, fashioning fish hooks out of needles, and how to tie flies on them to represent aquatic insects hatching from streams and lakes where trout lived. Also, the book presented the first dozen patterns for trout flies in English. In bringing fly fishing to the Church and ultimately to the public, Dame Julianna gave anglers reasons to study the foods that trout feed on and, thus, the habitats that trout live in. This brought about man's questioning of his influence on the habitat that he shared with trout.

During Dame Juliana's time, all the best fishing water was privately owned. The title "Dame" is the female equivalent of a Sir for knighthood, an honorific status in the aristocratic order. She was high born, giving her special privileges with both the church and estates owning all water rights. Therefore, she could fish in the best places without having to compete with the public. We can only guess what Dame Juliana's opinions would be in regard to current public access rights. She might be in favor of, or she might be appalled at, our management system. I think she would be a little of both. I also think I would like to be someone she would gladly share her water with. No doubt she would be an entertaining companion to fly fish with. I am sure we would see much of the world from differing perspectives. That would be fine. Fly fishing would be our bond, and we would probably learn much from each other. The first thing we might have to learn is how to be equals, and that would depend on whether we were transported to her time or mine.

It could be either time, but I hope we can meet in my time. I think her time was pretty stinky and very depressing.

In the six centuries since 1400 A.D., hygiene, medicine, rapid transit, and communication have become common. Scientific investigations have revealed that planet Earth is not flat. It is a sphere; the western half being discovered after 1400. Neither is the Earth the center of the Cosmos, as was widely believed. Earth orbits a star we call the Sun. Also discovered is our Solar System: Sun, Earth, and the seven other planets orbiting our Sun. Our solar system is only a speck in an indiscernible, vast universe of trillions of other specks. We had to consider that we may not be unique or important to any life beyond our own atmosphere. Contrary to the six-day creation doctrine, producing the current universe with humans may have taken thirteen and a half billion years.

As our knowledge base has expanded, our questions have become more complex. We demanded and received universal education. We were also granted the responsibility to think for ourselves and participate in governing decisions. Progress seems to be an eternal conflict between lessons of the past and visions of a future. In our current society, which originated from thirteenth-century Europe, the cultural roles of males and females have undergone significant changes. Males and females have become more equal, and imagining it any other way is challenging.

What makes the Treatise so remarkable is that with all the changes in technology and worldview, the basic beliefs about sport fishing are as relevant today as they were five hundred years ago. In 1957, author John McDonald helped us all discover the Treatise in his book, "The Origins of Angling." With translations from Old English into modern English, current-day readers can understand Dame Julianna's writings and command a wider worldview by placing themselves in her time. Any time you feel wimpy and think there is little opportunity for you, and you don't feel you fit in, or have no personal power, transport your mind to 1400 and imagine your surroundings. Doing so has made me more appreciative of the time I was born into. At least we were granted the gift of hope. And it is with hope this book is written.

Chapter 3

The Spark is Blown West

"Of course, I believe in free enterprise but in my system of free enterprise, the democratic principle is that there never was, never has been, never will be, room for the ruthless exploitation of the many for the benefit of the few."
-Harry S. Truman

There is evidence that Europeans had sailed to North America for several hundred years before Christopher Columbus made his famous voyage in 1492. Columbus's discovery opened the Caribbean to Spanish colonization and the New World to conquistadors such as Hernan Cortes. Gold was, and still is, the basis and measurement of power. Upon hearing rumors of gold, Cortes and his gang came to America in search of it. They then proceeded to sack the Aztec Empire in 1521. The flow of gold from Cortes's conquest initiated a stampede of European adventurers to the Americas. As men moved west from Europe into the new hemisphere, they found rich land inhabited by stone age cultures. All the European countries had gunpowder, horses, and steel. Might is always right. Superior European technology enabled many countries to establish colonies in this new world, all of which ultimately rebelled and won independence. A portion of the English colonies won independence and then declared manifest destiny. They took the whole middle third of North America for themselves. They evolved a new form of government based on English Common Law and the codes of the Iroquois Confederacy. Eventually, this new country, The United States, reached from the Atlantic to the Pacific Oceans.

A commercial fishery existed on the Columbia River for several thousands of years before Oregon became a state. Native Americans had harvested salmon from the rivers and processed them for trade by smoking, and drying the meat, then grinding it and packing it into special salmon skin lined willow baskets, some of which may have traveled over a thousand miles east to the Mississippian Culture. Both Europeans and Native Americans had the ambition to acquire wealth for themselves and their people. By this time, the European worldview was much larger, and harvesting and shipping technologies were much more efficient than the North American stone age cultures. Europeans had the means to transport salmon to global markets which were unavailable to Native Americans.

American Ship Captain Robert Gray discovered the mouth of the Columbia River, May

11, 1792. This lead to the U.S. Government to sponsor the Lewis and Clark Expedition who explored the lower Columbia River in 1805-1806. European exploration of the Pacific Coast of North America had started in the 1770s by both the Spanish and the British. Yet, west coast fisheries remained nearly untouched by European descendants for the next fifty years until the mid-1860s. There was huge demand for edible meat across the globe. Meat from salmon was very nutritious but spoiled easily. Europeans had fermented, dried, salted, and froze many kinds of fish, including salmon. Unfortunately, none of these methods proved dependable for long distance transportation. In 1864 vacuum-packed tinned cans supplied the final piece of the puzzle. Long-lasting vacuum-packed cans allowed salmon flesh to arrive in most parts of the world in deliciously edible condition. Capitalizing on this canning and transportation technology, European descendant commercial fishers, canners, and shippers nearly brought Pacific Salmon to extinction in the eleven years between 1864 and 1876. Some runs of the most in-demand Chinooks were extinct before 1870.

Under the stroke of President James Buchanan's pen, Oregon became the 33rd state in this American Union on Valentine's Day, 1859. Oregon was ceded all waters within its borders.

Which meant that the people in common owned all waters. All waters large enough to float a boat of any kind were deemed navigable, a huge change from the European model. It also meant that anything swimming in the water was exploitable by anyone with enough capitol and daring to do so. Oregon became a state just before the Civil War. During the Civil War, it was a backwater. In the ensuing fifty years after the American Civil War, Oregon and the rest of the nation experienced explosive growth and near-unlimited potential to provide staggering wealth to men of vision, courage, and ambition.

In 1875 the salmon runs crashed. Please keep this sentence in mind: *In 1875, the salmon runs crashed.* We have heard that phrase again several times in the last forty years. In the best of times, Pacific Salmon and Steelhead runs can vary widely in annual numbers of returning fish. A consortium of commercial fishing interests organized to find a solution and contacted the U.S. Fish Commissioner, Spencer Baird. Baird sent a young Harvard graduate biologist, Livingston Stone, to investigate the predicament. Stone toured the Columbia Basin in 1876 and offered two solutions. He proposed salmon sanctuaries and salmon hatcheries. Industrial- minded commercial fishers rejected the salmon sanctuary solution as being too restrictive but chipped in $21,000 for a hatchery. The first salmon hatchery in the Columbia Basin was built on Clear Creek, a Clackamas River tributary at Carver Park. An unseasonable September rain flooded the creek and washed away part of the hatchery and all the first year's production. Anadromous fish hatcheries have had a checkered history, but most remain in production to date.

Americans have always been good at asking themselves, "can we?", but never as conscientious about asking, "should we?" on the merit of many questions. American optimism demands all answers are yes! Naysayers are labeled as pessimists (then that word is translated to losers) because they slow down progress and profits. But because of this "we can" conscientiousness, some runs of the most in-demand Chinook Salmon were extinct before the first hatcheries or hydroelectric dams were built. But it turns out that hatcheries and dam builders became great business allies.

When the first dams were built, they all had a negative impact on what anadromous fisheries were left. Impassable dams eliminated masses of habitat from anadromous salmonids and disallowed recovery of overharvested salmon runs. (A few examples will be shown in the next chapter).

Salmon and Steelhead love steep, fast-flowing rivers, which are also preferred for generating electricity. This placed dam builders and commercial fishermen against each other as competing economic interests. Hatchery men offered a solution; electric companies would fund hatcheries with money for mitigating the loss of natural fish production caused by dams, and ratepayers would foot the bill. Later, sports fishermen, a newer user group, were forced to fund hatcheries through fishing license fees. Naturally, the commercial fishermen agreed to this unproven solution. All they wanted were fish to harvest at no cost.

Be forewarned some of the following paragraphs are going to sound pessimistic. They are merely observations, sometimes with offered solutions. I am not unbiased. I love our native fish and I love fly fishing; therefore, I study and research. And as Joe Walsh said in his self-examining song, *Life's Been Good*, "I'm just looking for clues at the scene of the crime." It is doubtful any North American salmonids will go extinct at the species level, but many subspecies have already gone extinct, and the current civilization should be informed. We have forced everything in the world to adapt to us, and every one of us is responsible. I believe everything in the Universe is connected. We all adapt to each other, and we all affect each other, as all parts of the

Universe in some way adapt to all other parts. The fish don't know that they are threatened or endangered. They probably have no ability to even conceptualize such abstract ideas as the future or loss. On this planet, it is only we who can calculate the unseeable. The pain of loss is only our own. It may be time to come to terms with our **lack of God-like power**. It is unlikely that we have the power to create devastation like the great lava floods that happened in the Columbia River basin seventeen million years ago, or the giant flood of water from the melting ice caps at the end of the last glacial epic, nor can we drop the Ocean level four hundred feet as it was during the last glacial maximum. The lineage of all the local salmon and trout survived all such traumatic events, but in my mind, there is little doubt they all went extinct in some places at some times. Change is inevitable. Everything changes every second of every day. Do not fear it. You cannot stop it but do not hesitate to influence it with your wit and your grit. You cannot help but do good just by thinking about it.

Everything in nature has natural cycles. Many of these cycles are poorly understood. Some cycles may as yet be undetected. Long before we white folks arrived, the red folks had various traditional dances and ceremonies to bring the salmon runs back to their river. In some beliefs, salmon were the souls of their ancestors returning to nourish their children. In the chain of life, it actually sounds reasonable. It seems plausible that these native cultures had suffered through some lean years of depleted fish runs. Or maybe their ancestors might not have been listening and did not return for some years. It had probably happened often enough to give the natives the suspicion that the ancestor could be influenced. If this hypothesis is valid, maybe the recent declines in some stocks may not be all our fault. It may, in part be the fault of our ancestors as well. It is hard to change the past.

Don't rejoice yet; we are not off the hook. There are some things that we should have guilt about (the other half can now rejoice because they are allowed to feel guilt). Damn right! Some of you should feel guilty as hell! Yes, you know who you are. You are the person who drained a wetland and built a housing project which put people and fish at risk, and/or used barbed trebles in a catch and release wild fish area, and/or dredged the river to allow your grain to get to market cheaply and then allowed your agricultural herbicides and pesticides ruin the water quality, and/or had a river channelized to save your trophy waterfront home. The devil has his crosshairs right in the middle of your center mass. Your only redemption is to pray deeply…. for salvation.

Chapter 4

The Power of Electricity

"We will make electricity so cheap that only the rich will burn candles."
-Thomas A. Edison

A logical assumption would be that the electrification of The United States of America started on the east coast in big cities such as New York or Boston. It did but it was localized. Another assumption could be that the Midwest was first because of Chicago's World's Fair in 1893. It was powered by George Westinghouse's generators using alternating current, perfected by Nikola Tesla. However, it wasn't the first. The first long-distance power lines ran from a powerhouse at Willamette Falls in Oregon City, Oregon, fourteen miles north. These lines powered fifty-five streetlights in downtown Portland on June 3, 1889. By the end of that year, those lines were supplying 4,000 volts to the city. Because of its geographical location at the mouth of the Willamette, where it joins the Columbia River, Portland became a progressive business center for hydroelectric expansion for the Pacific Northwest. Before Oregon became a state, the Falls on the Willamette had been a power source for water wheels. They powered woolen, grain, and lumber mills. It became a natural location to install turbines to turn generators. Several smaller rivers draining the rainy west slope of the Cascade Mountains were also tapped for hydroelectric power. The Columbia Watershed, the steepest river basin of that size in the world, was turned into the most dammed river on the planet before 1970. These projects produced enormous wealth for the nation. Adversely though, they contributed to the destruction of the world's best salmon-producing habitat on an industrial scale.

Not surprisingly, electric power and transportation companies found mutual commonality in the early 1900s. Both industries used emerging technologies. Using the same rights-of-way, they provided practical support for growing industries and the large population over huge geographical expanses. A steam engine locomotive could replace 1,000 horses for long-distance transportation. But electric motors were cleaner and quieter for inner city trolley cars. Electric lights were safer and brighter than any solid or liquid fuel could provide. Much like railroads, electricity needed vast capital, leading to easily formed monopolies over huge geographic areas.

Portland Railway, Light and Power Company owned street cars. They gobbled up and merged smaller businesses around the fast-growing metropolis of Portland. Capitalized by east coast money in the amount of $15 million, a staggering amount at the time, PRLP strived for consolidation and standardization of both rail transportation and electrical power. One of the smaller companies it acquired in 1912 was The Mt. Hood Railway Company, which owned transit services in East Multnomah County. They originated the development of dams and an electric generation station in the Sandy River Basin, which drains the west slope of Mt. Hood and the surrounding Cascade Mountains. The Sandy River proved to be difficult to harness.

Her steep gradient, coupled with torrential rainfall and glacial melt in the headwaters, gave the river an explosive and fluctuating nature.

The first two wooden dams built on the Sandy River failed. There is little historical record of these dams, but the wreckage of one of them is upstream about a quarter mile from the 2007 dam removal site. It appeared to have been a wooden crib with a bolted round log framework. I am assuming a winter storm had breached it. The preceding dam had probably been even cruder. When repositioned and re-engineered, the third dam finally held. It was anchored in a bedrock stratum, a wood crib of thick sawn timbers filled with heavy, angular basalt rocks keyed together. It was fifty yards long and fifty feet tall.

The forebay filled to the lip of the spillway with gravel provided by the river's annual bedload shift. It was called Marmot Dam, named after a small local community on the nearby Barlow Road part of the Oregon Trail. Marmot Dam headed a concrete-lined diversion canal paralleling the river for a couple of miles. Then, this water entered a tunnel through the Devil's Backbone Mountain Ridge and emerged slightly upstream of a second dam on the Little Sandy River. A wooden flume combined the flows of both rivers and transported the water seven miles to a holding pond called Roselyn Lake. From there, the stored water dropped three hundred feet in elevation through a couple of giant steel pipes called "penstocks" to twin generators on another tributary, the Bull Run River. There, the water was returned to the Sandy River eleven and one-half miles downstream from Marmot Dam. The dam was built with a fish ladder. Who knows why? We could find no evidence of a law requiring it. The same bedload shift that filled the forebay also plugged the ladder nearly every freshet, and there wasn't a screen on the diversion flume. Most juvenile fish migrating toward the ocean took this path, migrating down the flume to Roselyn Lake and ultimately going through the penstocks. They were hacked to pieces by the turbine blades that spun the generators.

Before 1939 there weren't any laws governing dam construction or the environmental impact of dams. The United States was a laissez-faire economy. If you could afford it, you could own it and run it without government interference. It didn't matter if it was a river to turn generators, trees for logging, land clearing for farming, grass for grazing, or fish for netting. There weren't any laws giving rights to the natural world. The wreckage of the fishery on the Sandy River has suffered through all of the above.

Logging, land clearing, and hydroelectric development also had tragic impacts on fisheries in adjacent drainages. On the Clackamas River to the southwest, a ladder less sawmill dam blocked all fish passage near the confluence with the Willamette River for twelve straight years, and a series of hydroelectric dams still impact fisheries there. On the Hood River drainage adjoining the Sandy Basin on the northeast, the Power dale Dam, water diversion and hydroelectric generation stations were very similar to Marmot in what was then termed the Bull Run Project. During the same historical period the Bull Run River, a lake-fed tributary that contributed a third of the flow to the Sandy River, was dammed for Portland's municipal water supply. This effectively ended this tributary's anadromous fishery forever.

The Marmot Dam on the Sandy River and its attached infrastructure had the capacity to divert more water than was in the river for over three months per year, which it did. The river dried up every summer in the eleven-and-a-half-mile section from the dam to the mouth of the Bull Run for sixty years. In the ensuing years, the progeny of fish that had spawned upstream of the dam went down the flume and was devoured by the generators. To prevent the annihilation of juvenile fish, the ladder was blocked. A hatchery was operated at the dam's base, but it got few returns. By the 1940s, all anadromous fish runs went functionally extinct in all the tributaries upstream of the dam. The ladder remained closed from 1939 to 1962, 23 years. Finally, in the early 1950s, residents gathered at the local pharmacy in the town of Sandy and petitioned for the intake of the flume to be screened. PGE, who then owned the dam, did so. The impact was immediate. If one can believe the records, the fish ladder was reopened in 1962 and there were 3,200 Winter Steelhead that went through the new counting station. The origin of these fish and the accuracy of the counts are not clear. Chinook runs were much less fortunate. Fall Chinook runs were hanging on in the lower Sandy, but Spring Chinook, which spawned in the upper basin, showed few signs of recovery.

This is a short, superficial, and abbreviated story about three small adjacent tributary watersheds in what is a vast watershed of the Columbia River Basin, a microcosm of the Columbia watershed itself. The watersheds of rivers are like trees, with the main stem being the trunk and the limbs being the tributaries. When a limb is cut, it doesn't affect the tree very much. But if you eliminate all the limbs and then turn the trunk into logs, all that is left is a dead stump. In the 1970s, The Association of Northwest Steelheaders produced a movie about the Columbia River called "Dammed Forever." It claimed at the time that there were 1,800 dams in the watershed. Dams serve many purposes: traffic & transportation, hydroelectric generation, flood control, and water storage & withdrawal for municipal & irrigation. Anyone's purpose results in a negative influence on anadromous fisheries. Most dams serve more than one purpose, and many serve all purposes. Could the current civilization exist without electricity? Certainly not! Electricity runs our civilization: entertainment, communication, refrigeration, heating, lighting, water supplies, and military defense. It enables and manages nearly everything. Can the current civilization exist without anadromous fish? Many people don't think or care about them. They are leftovers from the ice ages, evolutionary artifacts on the way to extinction. Let us not forget, our paths paralleled theirs through the same ice age. They may be canaries in our own coal mine. It looks like we are trying to put it to the test. Can I survive without anadromous fish? I don't want to try. I want to have my computer, and all my conveniences which run on electricity and many more anadromous fish too. Smart people shouldn't have to trade this for that! Long range planning should create balance. God gave us dominion. I read it somewhere. Why settle for less than was offered? I want to have it all! I want to have all the conveniences of the modern era and have plentiful runs of anadromous fish too! I need it now! I deserve it because God loves me!

Chapter 5

Leave the World Better

"Everyone who got where he is has had to begin where he was."
– Robert Louis Stevenson

At age eleven, I asked my mother what she wanted me to be when I grew up. I expected her to say something like a doctor, a lawyer, or a leader in government. Instead, she replied that I should figure out what I liked to do and then find a way to make a living doing it, and above all, she hoped her son would leave the world a better place than he found it. I took her wishes to heart but found the word "better" to mean different and often opposing things to different people. The word "better" can be an adverb, a noun, or a verb; in all forms, it is subjective, not quantitative, and may not be proven scientifically.

My father was drafted and stationed in Normandy when I was born in 1944. He and my mother ensured she was pregnant before he boarded a liberty ship for Europe, and they ensured I knew it as soon as I could understand. I was wanted. I was planned. I was the proof if dad didn't come home. My birthday is July 17, a water sign and I was born to be around water. My family name is Bachmann. In Swiss-German, Bach means water. The name translates to water man or the man who lives by the water. Water is essential to all life as we know it. I was drawn to water and fishing from my earliest times, especially fly fishing.

When WWII ended, my parents bought a small home on fourteen acres near Willamina, Oregon. For them, it was an interim place to live while searching for a home they really wanted. From there, my father boarded a Greyhound bus and toured Northern Idaho, where he purchased eighty acres. As soon as we moved to Idaho, he bought an adjoining eighty-acre parcel. The property was L-shaped. A medium size stream called Grouse Creek flowed in one end of the L and out the other. That gave us a lot of private water, which happened to be the best mile of the entire creek, and it wasn't just any old creek. Grouse Creek was the primary spawning water for the giant Kamloops and Bull Trout of the Lake Pend Oreille system, which at the time held the record for both species (Kamloops = 37 ¾ lbs. and Bull Trout 32 lbs). Composed of two combined farms, our place had two complete sets of buildings. The main creek system staging pool was thirty feet behind our second barn. Standing on a rung of a wooden ladder nailed to the inside wall of the haymow, I could survey the bottom of the whole pool by peering through the cable passage opening under the roof's peak thirty feet above the water. I often saw five to twenty trout over twenty pounds, and some might have weighed over thirty.

There was a road on our property that led to the creek. At first, we let people come and go as they pleased, but after some people abused the access, my father built a heavy plank gate and locked it. Three anglers had fished our property since they were kids. They all appeared to be related and called each other by nicknames: Jiggs, Punk, and Pops. Jiggs and Punk were probably in their thirties. Pops was in his sixties, retired, and kind enough to take a ten-year-old kid under his wing and teach him about fishing. My Dad figured he could trust them and gave each a key to the gate with instructions they could come and go individually or together but never share their privileges or keys with anyone else.

All three of these anglers fished fly gear. Which in the 1950s consisted of a bamboo fly rod with an automatic fly reel and silk fly line. It was an era when bamboo was being replaced by fiberglass as rod-building material. I remember Jiggs showed up one morning with a fancy- looking, white fiberglass Shakespeare Wonder Rod. Everyone wanted to try it. In a couple of weeks, Punk had one too. Pops liked his bamboo rod and thought the glass rods were funny looking. Jiggs, Punk, and Pops all fished jarred cured salmon eggs with the split shot when the river was high and dirty with snow melt, but they switched to flies when the river was clear. They took little notice of me for the first year, probably because I didn't have a rod or reel.

In Northern Idaho, young Tamarack trees grew so thick that they were exceedingly tall, straight, and skinny with very few limbs. If cut in the early spring, they were easy to peel. We always had a bundle of them drying and curing in the attic of the barn. These cured saplings were less than a quarter of an inch thick at the tip, twelve to fifteen feet long, and about the diameter of an adult male's thumb at the butt. When well cured each was like a bamboo cane pole, but much more substantial. We rigged them with a braided line, a four-foot-long, eight-pound test monofilament leader, a single hook, and a split shot. Usually, a garden variety angle worm was impaled on the hook and drifted next to the bottom of the creek with the speed of the current. These rigs were deadly for Cutthroats and other trout, up to five pounds.

It was with this kind of outfit that I caught my first trout. The creek was high and dirty with spring snowmelt. Dad, Jiggs, and Punk left me at the Barn Hole while they went upstream. The Barn Hole was formed by Grouse Creek colliding with and digging out a tree that had sunk into the bottom of an ancient glacial lake. The top and middle of the tree were anchored firmly under the barn. The base and root wad of the long-dead tree protruded from the bank and into the pool perpendicular to the current flow. During the lowest flows, the uppermost parts of the tree were more than two feet deep. The trunk above the roots was around four feet in diameter, with about a foot and a half of water flowing under it. Beyond that, the deepest roots were still buried in the stream bottom. The pool was fifty yards wide and over a hundred yards long in normal flows. The water was more than ten feet deep at the deepest point downstream of the tree. The muddy water entirely hid the submerged tree, but I knew exactly where it was and cast my worm to sink directly downstream. There the worm rested lightly on the bottom for a few seconds. Then there was a gentle tug as a fish picked up the worm. I raised the rod, felt resistance, and struck hard, slinging the fish high in the air behind me, where it hit the high barn wall and fell stunned but wiggled frantically into the thick green grass. In seconds, the seventeen-inch Cutthroat trout was in my grip, and I killed it by bashing his head against the barn wall. As a kid growing up on a farm, it was common to carry a pocketknife and learn how to use and maintain it early in life. When the three adults returned a few minutes later, my razor-sharp, single-blade knife had already removed the guts and gills. It was the only fish caught that day.

My father had little interest in fishing. At ten, my mother was afraid I would drown in the creek and wouldn't let me go fishing alone. However, in celebration of my first trout, my grandmother bought me a cheap mail-order fiberglass fly rod, reel, and line. I told Pops about it, and he took me fishing. At first, he would let me fish ahead of him, then come along behind me and catch all the fish. After a while, I would fish a section of water, circle around, and watch his technique. Pops were deadly. He fished wet flies upstream like dry flies, dead drift under the surface. He carried a leather fly wallet with felt pages. In it were three fly patterns: Gray Hackle Peacocks, Brown Hackle Peacocks, and Royal Coachman Feather Wing Streamers, all were size six. In those days, every angler carried a wicker creel on an over-the-shoulder harness.

All harvested trout and whitefish were butchered as soon as they were landed and layered inside the creel with vegetation between the layers. Brake ferns were the best layering material. Cleaned and layered this way, fish never got soft or spoiled during a day's fishing. Fishing was considered leisure time, but a home-bound angler was also expected to bring home fish for the table. However, living on a ranch with cattle, goats, hogs, and chickens, we always had protein. The farm-raised meat was stored in a couple of large freezers. We figured out in a hurry that fish that had been frozen were less palatable than the freshly caught ones. A half-full creel every other week was a treat. A full creel each week was drudgery. I learned the catch and release ethic not because of any conservation responsibility or because it became a socially popular ethic but because trout were a delicacy in specific numbers. If stored in a freezer, they weren't as good to eat. When we wanted fish to eat. I knew where they lived and harvested only as many as needed. This way, none got wasted.

When I was thirteen, I bought a Johnson Century closed-face spinning reel. I figured out that it could be modified to mount on a fly rod upside down like a fly reel on my fly rod. So, I loaded it with a twenty-pound test monofilament line and went hunting for larger trout. This rig gave me a lot more range. I showed it to Pops, and although he didn't say so, I could tell he immediately disliked it. So out of respect, I never used it when he was around.

My formative years in Northern Idaho were during the 1950s and early 1960s. Lake Pend Oreille was at its peak. When I was a kid, it held the world record for Bull Trout: a thirty- two-pounder caught by N. Higgins in 1949. Bull trout were native there.

It also had the world record for rainbow trout, a thirty-seven-pound twelve-ounce monster Kamloops caught by angler Wes Hamlet in 1947. Kamloops were not native to the Lake Pend Oreille basin. The Pend Oreille River exits the lake at Sandpoint, Idaho, and flows west toward Spokane, Washington, then north into British Columbia, where it joins the Columbia River. Just east of the Idaho-Washington border, the Pend Oreille River plunges over the edge of a granite ridge, forming an impassable barrier called Albeni Falls, which blocked all salmon and steelhead migration. Even though Steelhead were in the Columbia River upstream of the junction with the Pend Oreille River, they had yet to enter Lake Pend Oreille. Kamloops, along with Kokanee salmon, arrived there from the Kootenay Lakes area via a hatchery program around the start of World War II. The Kamloops and native Bull Trout fed on the Kokanee and grew to tremendous size, and both species migrated through my section of Grouse Creek. Many sizes of trout came up that creek. Some would feed a family all the fish they wanted to eat for a month. The largest Kamloops I landed out of that creek was when I was about fourteen. It weighed twenty-seven and three-quarter pounds on a feed scale with the guts and gills out of it.

I graduated from Sandpoint Senior High

School in 1962. I never inherited the agricultural gene, and even though I had a great set of parents and had grown up in paradise, the feeling was one of constraint. After working the winter of 1963 in a plywood mill in Libby, Montana, for the winter of 1963, I decided to return home. I stopped at a feed store on the way through Bonners Ferry and bought seven cases of ditching powder (dynamite) with the idea to drain a swamp my dad had wanted to turn into a hay field. On arrival home, mom informed me they had just sold the farm and were moving back to Oregon. It was a shock and a letdown. They went to Oregon and I stayed in Idaho. I met a beautiful red-headed girl named Bev, and after playing around with her for several months, she told me she was pregnant. So, I married her because it was an honorable thing to do and became the fly caught in the spider's web.

During the warm parts of the year, I had a good job building and maintaining hiking trails for the Kaniksu National Forest. During the cold months, though, even at the lower elevations, everything was covered with two to six feet of snow. In the early 1960s, it was common to work from April through October and draw unemployment from November through March. In mid-December, Bev and I traveled south to visit my parents, who had bought a house outside of Estacada, Oregon. I hunted around for work without much success. Then the weather turned bad. It snowed every day for a couple of weeks. By Christmas, there was a couple of feet of snow near sea level and twelve feet of water ladened snow at six thousand feet. Then came the Pineapple Express, the Jetstream that brought an atmospheric river from the South Pacific to the Pacific Northwest. Snow had been falling for weeks in the mountains, then the freezing level skyrocketed to eighteen thousand feet, and it rained twelve inches in twenty-four hours. Suddenly every tiny creek became a raging river, and rivers swallowed towns and cities. Houses, bridges, and roads disappeared. People were stranded. Electricity was out, water and sewer systems were obliterated, and much of the transportation system was washed away. There was chaos everywhere. The Pacific Northwest was declared a national disaster area. Suddenly work was abundant for people who could run machinery, build bridges, or drive trucks. I went to work for the Mount Hood National Forest rebuilding bridges and roads in the upper Clackamas River Drainage. Eventually, I was transferred to the Sandy River watershed based at Zig Zag to rebuild bridges, culverts, and roads and channelize rivers and streams. I found year round work in Oregon, bought a house, and we became Oregonians.

Our arrival in Oregon was two weeks before the worst flood in a hundred years. The 1964 Christmas Day Flood was nothing short of a cataclysm. There wasn't any time to contemplate the workings of nature or right or wrong according to any principle. Everyone was living in the past, trying to repair and regain what had been lost in the flood, never questioning if what had been was even logical or realistic.

The Sandy River drops six thousand feet in fifty-five miles. The Lolo Pass Road crosses the Sandy River at Zig Zag, where the naturally braided channel is wide and flat. At this point, the river drops in elevation forty-five hundred feet in eleven miles. This steep terrain creates extremely fast flows when the river is in flood. Here the river tends to meander and change channels over a wide distance. Groves of two-foot diameter trees standing over a hundred feet tall can be like wheat before a scythe during peak floods. But it was debris from floating house parts that took out most of the bridges in the upper Sandy River Basin. In 1964, the flooding Sandy washed out a long stretch of the Lolo Pass Road and stranded many people. The only transportation across the river for a month was a cable car, but few people involved learned much. This scenario happened again in 1996. In the thirty-two years between the two floods, legal setbacks were designed to remove houses from the river riparian zone and from harm of floods. After 1996, the zoning of building setbacks was supposedly strengthened. As this book is being written, building permits are still being issued in wetlands and floodplains. There is little that compares to the tenacity of some developers. Along with realtors, they are some of the *shortest-term profit* motivated people in any nationhood. This sector works very closely with community planners. Developers attend every meeting and nudge things their way continually. Environmentalists tend to enjoy making a big deal out of a cause, stirring public sympathy for their point of view, getting a law passed, and then trusting the government to provide enforcement out of the common treasury. Nearly every public official will see this as a net loss. That person now has to spend the same amount and create more work for themselves. At the heart of the conflict is: the "rights of the many vs. the rights of the few." Both sides have used concise terminology defining what they believe is important. Private property rights vs. land-use issues are each considered to be a key management tool for ***leaving the world a better place***. Often the terms lead to completely opposite conclusions on how to manage a river. Often the opposition to wider buffer zones is the loss of tax revenue. Maybe instead of spending thousands of dollars on creating artificial log jams from logging debris, we might spend the same money on preventing the next generation of log jams from being made from the debris of flooded waterfront homes. But then insurance companies couldn't collect so much money while betting the next big flood won't happen within our lifetimes. From my recent observations, the way homes are lined up on the waterfront of the upper Sandy River basin, a 1964 flood type of event will involve a lot of private residences, and wealth lost….and some will say, "Why didn't somebody do something?" And someone else will say, "I guess we already did. And it was by committee and by popular consensus."

Chapter6

Budding Environmentalists

"To be yourself in a world that is constantly trying to make you something else is the greatest accomplishment."

-Ralph Waldo Emerson

Growing up on a small cattle ranch in Northern Idaho, I had exclusive access to a premium trout stream. There were no reasons to question fishery practices or land use management. I was a purely red, white, and blue capitalist, or at least thought so. Fate intervened when I moved to Oregon, where I became involved in building bridges, installing culverts, and channelizing rivers. I learned that cold-water fishery habitat is incredibly fragile there, and most people didn't know or care about it. There was something about operating a giant track-driven machine while turning a beautifully braided natural river into a straightened, V-shaped ditch to protect a bunch of waterfront vacation homes, which led me to evaluate my impact on the natural environment. I started to be aware that maybe the river's health was more important than the buildings. Maybe it was poor judgment to build next to a river, and maybe the whole community was paying for the stupidity of a few landowners who had made poor choices. For a while, my thoughts wouldn't come into complete focus. It took more than that to wake me up completely. It also took the Vietnam War. I didn't serve or attend demonstrations against it, but U.S. foreign policy made me question, for the first time, the direction of what I still consider the best country ever on Earth. The shock of seeing how deeply the Vietnam War was ingrained into our government's decision-making apparatus made me start questioning its fundamental sanity. Watching how easily the general population followed along also made me take stock of the fragility of democracy itself. False gods and charismatic politicians are apparently easy for the blind to follow.

I was only becoming aware of this political situation when I joined the Sandy River Chapter of The Association of Northwest Steelheaders in 1967. My only intention for joining was to learn how to catch more Steelhead. After a few meetings, it became clear that it was mostly a social club, and I was already catching more Steelhead than most members. Being very protective of my own fishing, I kept my spots, techniques, and agenda under tight security.

It was during my second meeting that I realized the Steelheaders were more than a fishing club.

They were also concerned about conservation and fishery politics. They opposed Columbia River commercial gillnet fishing and were resisting the construction of Lower Granite Dam; the last dam being built on the Snake River. Preliminary construction started in July 1965. Every Steelheaders business meeting was rife with resentment toward this dam. I listened quietly and became more interested in each session that I attended.

Fast forward two years later to The Whistle Stop Tavern on Oregon Hwy 26, near the base of Mount Hood, Oregon's tallest volcano. It was a noisy, smokey, low-lit room. There were clunks of beer mugs, the thundering laughter of Herb Forbes, and the low-pitched growl of Freddy Gilbert in the background of any afternoon conversation. If you were looking for a quiet place to hang out, it wasn't The Whistle Stop. There was always something going on. There was an afternoon when Everett Nafts knocked out most of a guy's front teeth for insulting his wife. Several teeth, with attached gum lines, lay in the lint under the foosball table for most of a month. Then there was the time this skinny kid came through the door with a loaded .22 rifle and touched off a round into the ceiling. Before the kid could work the bolt to put another cartridge in the chamber, Freddy took the gun away, and hit him in the chest with the rifle butt, knocking the kid through the open front door. The kid scrambled to hide inside his car and locked the doors, thinking he was safe. In pursuit, Fred used the unloaded rifle to beat all the glass out of the vehicle until no wood was left on the gun. The windshield went first, followed by the back glass, the doors, and side windows, then the headlights and taillights. Fred threw what was left of the barreled receiver through the glassless windshield opening and screamed at the kid to get his piece of shit auto wreckage out of his parking lot and never to come back.

I don't want to give anyone the impression that the Whistle Stop was a rough or dangerous place. It was just the most popular community tavern for working-class people in a community that was fringy. From 1966 until 1990, the Hoodland community comprising Alder Creek to Rhododendron was energetic. There was lots of work to be had, and money was flowing. Flood damage was being repaired. Houses, roads, bridges, and the general infrastructure were getting lots of attention. Timber harvest provided a lot of jobs. The money trickled down. The area had a can-do attitude. With an active mind and strong muscles, anything might be possible. Hwy 26 was the Mt. Hood Hwy. The part from Rhododendron to Brightwood had been the Barlow Trail, the primarily covered wagon road segment of the road that took the main migration route between St. Louis, MO, and Oregon City. Between Rhododendron and Alder Creek, there were Brightwood and Wildwood. Each started as a campsite along the wagon trail. Each village had a local tavern. The Whistle Stop was between Brightwood and Wildwood. It had been built from scavenged secondhand railroad ties.

Freddy (Fred) Gilbert and his wife Virginia owned the Whistle Stop and had made it the most successful watering hole within the extended community. Fred, an ex-marine, was of average height, five eleven, but one of those narrow-waisted, barrel-chested, broad-back guys. He had massive arms and a short bullneck. They say once a jarhead, always a jarhead. Fred wore his flat top crew cut hair high and tight and always had a five o'clock shadow that masked the network of tiny veins in his cheeks. Fred spoke with a low, natural, easily audible growl, kind of like a bull alligator. He always wore blue jeans, lace-up boots, and a tee shirt, and often wore a white canvas bib apron complete with a change pocket containing a large, full dimensional, embroidered cloth penis which he was notorious for showing to certain female customers when making their change. The most charismatic thing about Fred was his overall honesty which gave him total fearlessness. He was a natural-born leader and the herd bull in any herd. He let people party as hard as they wanted to, but when he growled, "That's enough," people took him seriously. The Whistle Stop was out in the boondocks on a lonely highway and, after the sun went down, could have been a target for all kinds of nefarious acts, but none succeeded. Fred kept a long barrel, forty-four magnum Ruger Black Hawk revolver under the bar.

Fred was a rough and gruff type of guy, but he knew how to sell beer. The good-time people loved him. The room had a long, L-shaped bar with seating for fifteen, a dozen upholstered booths, a shuffleboard, a pool table, and a foosball table. The ceiling was finished with twelve-inch square fiberboard tiles. Each tile had a cardboard Heidelberg keg bung cover stapled in the center. Rumor was that Fred sold enough beer to fasten a bung cover in the center of all 1,200 tiles in less than a year. Between the bung covers were customer autographs from all over the world. Fred always left a couple of black felt markers on the bar for customers to use to write on the ceiling.

Fred's wife, Virginia, cooked, kept books and sometimes tended the bar. She seemed to be the perfect mate for Fred, his perfect team member. Virginia was made of the same rock- hard stuff as Fred, but where he was always the center of attention, she was reserved, very ladylike, yet very approachable. The relationship between them was evident. Fred made all the business decisions and had 97% of the contact with the customers. Virginia was the other alert set of eyes in the room; she knew her role, unquestioningly, totally solid backup. She also had a big-bore handgun hidden but within practical reach. I never knew her to point it at anyone.

Few people knew the place was armed. The Sixties and Seventies were peak decades for timber harvest from the Mt. Hood National Forest. There was a steady stream of log trucks on Hwy 26 from early in the mornings to late in the afternoons. During the summer months after 9:00 p.m., the road traffic died to nothing, and there was often a log truck pulling contests in the middle of the highway in front of the tavern. Looking back, it doesn't seem like fertile habitat for a budding environmentalist wanting to remove a dam. Many of the men involved had fought in WWII, the Korean War or Vietnam. Some had fought in all three. Conservation was a new thought to many, but the concept of taking care of their community was deeply ingrained, and each understood that either you ran the Government, or it ran you. A high percentage of loggers and construction workers were Steelhead fishermen. They lived and worked outdoors in a hazardous environment and were alert and intelligent enough to do so. They placed a high value on their fishery and were gutty enough to take on any adversary to protect it, especially since the leader of this conservation movement was one of their own. Or, in this case, two of their own.

Herb Forbes had just gotten out of the Army when I met him. His family owned a small house half a block from the Whistle Stop. From the time I met him, I gauged there was much more to Herb beyond his hearty laugh. First, he spoke fluent Russian, compliments of a language school paid for by the U.S. military. Second, Herb was always mysterious, trained by military intelligence in information acquisition. He was a master at laying down a smokescreen. You never knew what to believe. Some of his stories were outlandish, but every time I called bullshit, he was able to cover his tracks. Supposedly he got kicked out of Russia for spying. Who was to know? He looked like the pictures circulating of typical Russian men. Herb was about the same height as Fred and also was stocky. Herb was more average built with wavy blond hair cut to average length. Sometimes he wore a curly blond beard which he had trimmed every two weeks. Herb wore his blue jeans belted and nearly always had a plumber's crack showing if he bent over because he rarely tucked in the tail of his flannel shirt. Herb loved to laugh. If he was within a hundred yards, he was usually audible.

Herb and a couple of dozen other denizens of the Whistle Stop became a cast of characters for a long-term adventure play that would become a melodrama for half my life. But maybe I'm getting ahead of myself.

Chapter 7

Dynamite Politics

"In the game of life, a young man needs a dragon to slay for self-esteem. The audience sees the dragon slayer as a hero but rarely acknowledges the role of the dragon. No dragon, no story!"
--Mark Bachmann

The late 1960s were different than today. Environmentalists weren't always sweet- talking guys who volunteered for non-profits and organized fundraisers to support an Executive Director so crowds of socialites could dress up in tweed jackets or high heels and be seen bidding on expensive donations at a discount to make it look like they were doing something that actually protected wild fish. In the 60s, 70s, and early 80s, environmentalists were more inclined to get their hands dirty while spiking ancient trees to dismantle saw chains in an attempt to keep giant firs, spruce, and redwoods from being felled. Many activists emulated "The Fox." "The Fox" was the ghostly nemesis of polluting industries around the Great Lakes area. He capped off giant smokestacks and captured barrels of effluent from river polluters, then dumped it in their very own board rooms. The

Fox took credit for all the havoc he created by signing all his work "FOX," with the O being replaced by a drawing of a fox's head. He was never caught or named until after his death in November 2001. He was a hero to environmentalist organizations like Greenpeace and some members of the Sierra Club. But he was reviled by the industrial establishment as a terrorist. He was a modern, non-fictional Zorro.

Fish Conservation and Environmental Restoration weren't fashionable activities in the 1960s, 1970s, and 1980s. Environmentalists and conservationists were considered fringy if they thought rich families' waterfront cabins were not good for the ecosystem of a creek or river. Those who believe that someone's waterfront trophy home, built in a floodplain, is a hazard to the environment and an eye sore in the view shed is labeled as an extremist by the county property tax collectors. The wild fish cause is often lost not with regulators or lawmakers but with managers and enforcement. Some guys from my neighborhood were called Mount Hood Radicals by ODFW managers as late as 2000 for wanting barbless hook regulations installed in the upper Sandy River watershed to reduce trauma to wild fish. Conservation of wild fish species is now a mainstream cause to nearly everyone who features themselves as not being impacted. Widening riparian zone protection is fashionable on public land. The cause often remains popular for private land until you ask how many club members own a waterfront home. Defining the real causes of wild fish decline are still fringy subjects, but not as much as in the 1970s.

Deke was a local guy who revered The Fox as a role model. Deke showed up in the Mt. Hood Community in mid-1968 and wouldn't have stood out in any crowd. He was small, dark-complected with dark eyes and had a dark scraggly beard and hair. He wore work clothes everywhere he went and wasn't mindful of his hygiene. He introduced himself as a "fresh from

Vietnam, Army demolition expert." Deke confessed one night, when he was deep in his cups, that he wasn't proud of some of his assignments in Vietnam. He viewed parts of the U.S. Government as the enemy of man. He had signed on as a "powder monkey" with one of the local logging road construction outfits. Like many of the unmarried labor force of his day, a local tavern was a regular stop on his way home from work. He got swept up in the whirlwind of anti-dam sentiment at the Whistle Stop.

On a cold winter night, a dozen vehicles were in the margins around the darkened Whistle Stop. A tandem-drive flatbed truck rumbled in and parked in the shadows of tall firs at the edge of the dusty gravel parking lot. There was a loud hiss as the pneumatic parking brake was set. The noisy V8 engine shut down, and the twin stacks went silent. The driver's door creaked open, and a shadowy figure disembarked, walking around the truck, inspecting the tie-down straps holding a tarped load in place. The same dark figure crossed the space lit only by the faint light of a quarter moon. On the shadowed side of the building, a door opened, and the figure disappeared through it. It was midnight; the tavern had just closed.

The room was half full of people hanging on to their last beer. Deke strode through the back door and said, "The goods are in the parking lot. Two tons of dynamite, seven and a half tons of ammonium nitrate fertilizer, two hundred feet of fuse, and half a dozen blasting caps. I was at the dam today fishing. The gate to the flume will be locked open - a pair of bolt cutters will open the lock. That huge pile of over-burden from their construction project is still in place. The D-8 Cat is still parked there. We shut the water off in the flume. It will take half an hour to drain out, then we back the truck to the flume, unload the explosives into the flume, set the caps and fuses, cover the explosive with the dirt pile, light the fuses and leave. We will be about even with Cooks Ranch when the explosion happens. The charge will take out the intake to the flume and the north end of the dam."

It was like someone had poured a quart of ice water directly into my guts. Suddenly, I realized that what had been perceived as a bunch of drunken talk was no idle threat. This crazy bastard really had in mind to blow up Marmot Dam. Sitting against the wall in a booth with a half-full beer mug on the table, I replied, "You can't be serious!!?"

Deke was instantly disappointed. He hurled back, "You fuckin' right, I'm serious. There are nine and a half tons of explosives on a truck fifty feet from where you are sitting, and you think I ain't serious. You guys want to talk about getting rid of the dam. You are a bunch of talkers and dreamers. I have the means to make it happen! By the day after tomorrow, it will be gone!"

My reply came easily, "And two days after that, we'll all be in jail. This ain't Vietnam! The dam doesn't belong to the Vietcong. You ain't in the Army anymore. An hour after that explosion goes off, the FBI will be up your ass like a rubber hose. Everyone in this room will be complicit. Maybe they will let us out in twenty years, or maybe not. I want no part in it. My suggestion is that you take that truck to the rock quarry, and we forget this night ever happened!"

Herb said, "Mark's right; this is a bad idea."

There was grumbling in the background. A decision hung in the balance. Then Fred, standing behind his bar, concurred with Herb. "Yaa, this discussion never happened. I'm shuttin' her down. Everybody leaves now and go home! This Party is over!" So, it ended. The dam stood for many more years. I think that night, Freddy Gilbert's force of personality kept a bunch of hot heads from suffering in prison for many years.

On the other hand, if the dam had come out thirty-eight years earlier, the fishery might have been better off. All trails through life offer a myriad of opportunities and consequences. All we can do is hope we choose wisely and enjoy the experience.

A month later, someone dynamited a steel tower in the main transmission line on the north side of Mt. Hood, shutting down the Northwest Power Grid for several hours. No suspects were ever found. By that time, Deke had supposedly left the area for who knows where. It left me wondering.

Around this time, I read an article by Charles Ritz. He was an avid fly fisher who was very complimentary about a fly-fishing tackle retailer named Norm Thompson Outfitters of Portland, Oregon. The next time I was in Portland, I stopped by. I must have looked entirely out of place in my faded flannel shirt and blue jeans amid the tweed jackets and hand-knitted Norwegian sweaters. I talked about fly fishing with the man behind the counter, and it was like we were brothers, though he was at least twice my age. He gave me a hardcover copy of John McDonald's book "The Origins of Angling" and said Mr. McDonald would want me to have it. I have read and reread it many times, and it is now quite beat up. It is the modern interpretation of the book "A Treatise of Fishing with an Angel" written by a nun about sport fishing and is the first in the English language. It explains fly fishing and flies as they were known five hundred years ago. Every time I read it, I get this image of a lonely woman sitting at a table in a gloomy room, lit by a single smokey candle. She is working diligently with her inkwell and quill pen on a manuscript so that anglers in the far future will know about fly fishing and how it teaches people to respect trout and their environment. That candle, pen and fertile intellect produced a spark illuminating the minds of fly anglers through the ages. Reading the book taught me that fly fishing and fish conservation are interconnected. And the sport of fly fishing is more than five hundred years old. Having lasted for more than five centuries, the sport of fly fishing and its interpretive thoughts about nature are pursuits to follow.

In Dame Julianna's time there weren't many dams built. If there had been, there wouldn't have been much recourse against them. In today's world it might be more expedient to just blow up a dam without authorization. We chose to wait forty years for the rest of society to catch up. In the meantime, many non-profit organizations rose to the cause. By working with government agencies and dam owners, they made removing dams streamlined, legal and fashionable. Consequently, instead of taking out one dam, they removed hundreds of dams by the will of the people. Removing dams isn't fringy anymore.

Chapter 8

Taking Part in Democracy

"Your time is limited, so don't waste it living someone else's life. Don't be trapped by dogma which is living with the results of other people's thinking." --Steve Jobs

In 1969, The Association of Northwest Steelheaders took a lead role in opposing further construction on the Lower Granite Dam on the Snake River. It was about this time that Herb found out that the Marmot Dam on the Sandy River was due for relicensing through the Federal Power Commission (FPC). To that point, few of us had heard of this government agency that had issued PGE a 30-year license for the dam in 1940. Herb and I agreed that the correlation of these events was too good of an opportunity to pass up. The Association of Northwest Steelheaders became our affiliation of choice to oppose the relicensing. In November of 1969, we formed the Mt. Hood Chapter of The Association of Northwest Steelheaders. We started with twelve members and a mission statement to remove Marmot Dam from the Sandy River. At age twenty-four, I was proud to be elected as Chapter President, with Herb as Secretary. We had no realistic idea of what we were getting ourselves into. Within two years, our organization grew to over two hundred members in a community of 2,500 residents. We created a program to bring our case to the public. Herb and I spearheaded the publicity campaign. Freddy Gilbert and his close buddies, Moon Mullins and Dates Lymph, figured out how to raise money for a war chest. It wasn't easy. At every step, there were naysayers, "It won't work, never been done before, you will never get the dam removed, you can't fight city hall, you are up against too much money, are you fucking insane?!?, they asked.

We always believed that the Oregon Department of Fish and Wildlife was our natural ally. Maybe some factions were. But it turns out they were the minority. My assessment after the fact, 50+ years later, was that ODFW leadership was more interested in keeping the

$400,000 annual mitigation money instead of improving fish passage by removing the dam. *(Remember from Chapter-3): It turns out that hatcheries and dam builders became great business allies.* ODFW apparently threw up a few roadblocks to dam removal and hung on to prior agreements as long as possible. Of the twenty two stakeholders, ODFW was the last to sign the removal order, but maybe they were just being conservative.

Conservation of natural resources is that kind

of game. Most people join or form conservation organizations because of their ideals. Others form nonprofits because they think it is easy money. Based on what they say, it can be hard to tell who your real allies are. Many people do have honest scruples. However, some will pretend to be your ally because they fear you or they see an advantage for themselves if you win. These will deny being involved if you lose or attempt to take the credit if you triumph. In the movie TV series Shogun, the English navigator Blackthorn asked the Japanese Emperor Taranaga if there is ever a purpose for rebellion against a central authority. Taranaga replied, “Only if you win, otherwise you may lose your head.” We didn't realize the weight and size of our adversary, a publicly owned power company with government backing. It was a militarily strategic, power-generating apparatus with community dependence. The facility we were attacking provided enough electricity to light about 10,000 homes. Big public utility companies are woven right into the fabric of society. They are connected everywhere and to nearly everyone. But with perfect naivety, we dove right into the mix… the mouse that roared!

Herb and I figured that Marmot Dam was different from the Lower Granite because the Marmot Dam had already been in place for 55 years.

At the time, the Lower Granite was under preliminary construction. On the other hand, fish passage problems had persisted at Marmot Dam for its entire life. PGE was in the process of relicensing through a government agency that could be influenced by public opinion. I took pictures of the Marmot Dam during the summer when no water was flowing over it and the dry riverbed below the dam completely blocked fish passage. Herb's brother Rick worked at a photo outfit and blew up one of those pictures to a 4' X 6'. We built a showy red cedar folding display and used the picture as a centerpiece. In the framed panel above the picture, in foot-tall letters, it read, "Remove Marmot Dam from the Sandy River!" In one three-foot wide swing-wing panel, there was a complete map of the Marmot Dam complex. It showed the diversion canal, tunnel, Little Sandy Dam, flume, Roselyn Lake, generation station, and the Sandy and Bull Run Rivers. The other wing of the display told all about the history and operation of the facility, copied from PGE's official material. To that, we added our perspective on the impacts on the fishery and surrounding environment. We also had three-fold handout brochures printed, as well as some bumper stickers for sale printed with "Marmot Dam = Dead Fish." On the sticker, "Dead Fish" was replaced by a fish skeleton with an "X" through the eye. The lettering and fish were bright fluorescent orange on a black background. They cost us fifty cents to make, and we sold them for $3.95 apiece. We arranged with a dozen shopping centers in the region to set up our display and talk to people about the Marmot Dam. At first, we were apprehensive about how the general public would receive our information. Our first shopping center was on the east side of Portland. After a couple of hours on the first day, we were no longer apprehensive. Most people weren't familiar with the Sandy River and had never heard of Marmot Dam but became sympathetic to our cause in a very short time. They willingly accepted our brochures, and many also bought our bumper stickers. We had a righteous cause and a winning presentation. Within a month, there were hundreds of cars sporting our distinctive bumper stickers.

Meanwhile, Fred and his crew produced a fundraising plan that everyone supported. It was the Mt. Hood Seafood Festival. Most of the newly organized Mount Hood Chapter members were also Lion's Club members. The Lion's Club had a giant pavilion with a big professional kitchen. Fred donated a keg of beer and his OLCC license to run the tap. These boys knew how to throw a party the whole community would support. They contacted an Oregon oyster farmer who sold oysters by the gallon can. These community fundraisers netted thousands of dollars and made the dam removal club financially independent from any corporate sponsorship.

They also put together a program where a group of chapter members went on a shad fishing trip on the Lower Columbia River. They caught gunny sacks full of shad. Chapter member Elmer Erie had a giant smokehouse on his property at Sleepy Hollow, where several

hundred pounds of shad filets were cured. The smoked shad was then taken to a commercial canner and packed into one-pound tins. The Sea Food Festivals and the sales of canned shad provided the chapter with a healthy cash flow. The Mt Hood Chapter grew in a couple of years to be one of the largest in the Association of Northwest Steelheaders organization. The other large chapters were in large cities. Our chapter was in a tiny rural community of 2,500 scattered people. We had a cause that people could believe in because it was real and had been real for 55 years, and the destructive effects of the Marmot Dam were easy to display. It was only about sixty days after our chapter formation that PGE sent a man out to join our club, to keep an eye on us. His title was Fishery Biologist, but we figured him for a PR guy. When we shut down the chapter four years later, we donated our treasury to the Association of Northwest Steelheaders in the amount of over $20,000.

It was during this time that I read "The Greening of America" by Charles A. Reich, published in 1970, about people changing the world by becoming involved in environmental projects. It was this reading that got me questioning my own consciousness. Before that, I kept my eyes focused on mainstream trends, and I followed along. Even I, part of the rock-listening, blue jean-wearing crowd of free-thinking rebels, realized I was just following the group of status quo. As a heavy equipment operator, I was also following the money along its path of environmental destruction. "The Greening of America" fully opened my eyes.

Chapter 9

More than Sex, Drugs,

and Rock N' Roll

"It's time for our business and political leaders to redefine morality beyond sex, drugs, and rock and roll to include lying, hypocrisy and callous indifference to those in need."

--Arianna Huffington

There was no Summer of Love for me. I was not sensitive to the hippy movement or what it stood for until a couple of years later. After becoming aware of it and experimenting with it, I never became immersed in it. I owned a home and had kids, so the commune life had no appeal. I moved about fairly easily between most layers of society. In 1967 I was a WG-7 working for the US Forest Service, a public agency committed to the logging industry, and was busy building and maintaining roads so timber could be harvested efficiently. The late 1960s and early 1970s have a reputation among the top tier of American society as being all about drug abuse and rebellion. Mostly because many of them were too timid or arrogant to investigate the indicators of social change. Change of any kind frightens many people, "This is the way it has always been done. I don't care if my family kills fish and trees in Oregon; I'm spending my winter south of the Equator."

During the era of The Summer of Love, Woodstock, and Vortex, many second tier (middle class) citizens of the Pacific Northwest began to question whether the political establishment had the best plan for the natural world. Politicians were typically from the upper crust social class, the ones mostly responsible for over harvest and environmental destruction. Their environmental outlook was summed up in a song by Joni Mitchell, "You don't know what you've got 'til it's gone. They paved Paradise and put up a parking lot."

Oregon Governor Tom McCall (1967-1975) was a pragmatic environmentalist who read the pulse of the common man and spearheaded legislation that ushered in a new age in Oregon. McCall introduced measures such as the Oregon Beach Bill that guaranteed public access to beaches, DEQ monitoring and pollution laws enforcement, the Oregon Bottle Bill, cleaning our highways, and Vortex. This was an era of dynamic changes beyond subcommittees and board rooms, which gave the access of power to the people.

I attended Vortex, "A Biodegradable Festival of Life," commonly known as The Vortex Rock

Festival. It was held at Milo McIver State Park on the Clackamas River, near my home in Oregon. It was a state-sponsored event to circumvent a potentially violent clash at the American Legion National Convention in downtown Portland. In pure 1970s Oregon politics, Governor Tom McCall was by far the most levelheaded administrator this state has ever had. He and his inner circle got wind that several thousand war-protesting kids were coming to Oregon to bust up downtown Portland during the convention. Brilliantly, McCall invited the protestors to attend a Woodstock-like party. It had live bands with speakers that were so large they were set up on flatbed trucks on each side of the stage. It worked. Portland was saved from violence! The FBI estimated that 50,000 attended Vortex. McCall's critics declared it the "Governor's Pot Party." But most Oregonians decided it was "pure genius." There was something about skinny dipping in the beautiful Clackamas River with several hundred other like-minded people that took the hostility out of everyone. It was a way cool trip. What I do remember most is that despite the political risk taken and the brilliant tactics used, few were changed by Vortex. What it did do was draw attention to preserving the planet for forthcoming generations. War, pollution, and over-harvesting were not healthy or sustainable.

In 1970, Steelhead had never been categorized as a sport fish in Oregon. They and all species of Pacific Salmon were labeled the same, fish for both sport and commercial harvest. Steelhead had been declared gamefish in Washington State in 1969. Oregon and Washington share the Columbia River as a border for about three hundred miles. This meant that Steelhead could be illegally netted in the Washington half of the river and sold to legal buyers on the Oregon side, causing an enforcement nightmare, among other problems.

About this time, Walt McGovern, a Portland businessman, and Carey Starzinger, a biotech researcher, put together an organization specifically to get Steelhead designated as gamefish in Oregon. It was called the SORT (Save Oregon's Rare Trout) Committee. Carey Starzinger talked Herb and me into becoming lobbyists for the SORT Committee, who had fashioned five bills to be presented to the Senate Agriculture and Natural Resource Committee. We went to Salem, Oregon's state capital, and got acquainted with many state senators and representatives. It was exciting and heady work for a high school graduate, blue-collar country boy. One day Herb and I sat down in Governor Tom McCall's office for about half an hour. The Governor leaned back in his chair with his feet up on one side of his desk; Herb and I did the same on the other side. Tom McCall was a big man, about six foot four, and the single most charismatic individual I have personally ever met. We all agreed that the Columbia River was being over-harvested.

On specific days, the SORT Committee was allowed to make presentations to the Senate Agriculture and Natural Resource Committee. There were often large crowds of people in the room. There was always applause and much acclaim after our slick, well-organized and documented presentations, accompanied by promises to vote for our bills. Then every night, the commercial fishing interests would throw big parties with cases of whisky, helicopter rides, and pretty girls. The following day, our specific bill would get voted down. I remember during one session, a big Nordic-looking commercial fisherman got up and testified, "All them greedy sportsmen want to do is kill those fish while they are in the little creeks having their babies." At the time, I thought it was the dumbest thing I had ever heard, but it was definitely effective. The entire Senatorial Committee looked at us as if we were a mass gang of baby killers. The SORT Committee filed for a referendum and put the issue to the people's vote, and it passed; SORT Committee Measure 15 (1974), yes = 458,417 62%, no = 274,182 37% made Steelhead a game fish in

Oregon.

At about that same time, a PGE representative came to us and said that ODFW was working with PGE on a relicensing agreement for the Marmot Dam complex. The agreement entailed: minimum flows from the dam to the mouth of the Bull Run River to improve stream passage for fish, block load instead of the peaking power plant to minimize unnatural fluctuations in water level, improvement of the fish ladder for passage and counting, and improving flume screens to improve safety for downstream migrating juvenile fish. Our Steelheaders Chapter had mixed feelings but voted to accept these proposals. Our agreement made way for a hatchery summer Steelhead test- planting in the Sandy River headwaters in 1972. The fish returned in 1974, proving a summer Steelhead run was viable in the Sandy River Basin. In 1974, stocking programs of these fish started in earnest, with over 100,000 smolts planted in the watershed each year. Returns above Marmot Dam fluctuated between 1,500 to the highest return in 1988 of 7,800 adult steelhead. They averaged 6-20 lbs. each. From my point of view, it was one of the greatest freshwater sport fisheries I have ever encountered. It brought between 2-4 million dollars of economic stimulation (1970's dollars) to the small rural community that we lived in. Having lived in that same community before, during and after this program was introduced and then discontinued, I knew the monetary effects were very evident. Lindsay Wagner and Clint Eastwood each bought vacation homes within our community. I never met either one of those two people, but their Hollywood friends proved to be great tippers for fishing guides.

The runs of large numerous summer steelhead were only a facsimile of the real thing. The fish were real, but their large runs were only an illusion. Populations of giant sea run rainbows like them may or may not have ever existed naturally in these small clear headwater streams. If they had been there in large numbers, they would have been wiped out before being acknowledged by the current civilization.

I think the reason why the folks from Tinsel Town liked our fishery so much and decided to invest money in our community is that they were able to see it for what it was, an illusion like a movie strictly for entertainment and enjoyment. The way our civilization has treated the landscape, few watersheds are capable of supporting wild summer steelhead runs in fishable numbers. Most anglers are unable to afford to travel to remote places where wild summer steelhead still exists. It is kind of the same as most of us will never be heroes. But we can watch a movie and make believe we are handsome badass tough guys for a while. And many fishermen could catch a hatchery steelhead and make believe they, too, were rich guys. Our local community actively supported both wild and hatchery fish management (before, it was only one way or the other).

By 1974 we had achieved our primary goals with the Mt. Hood Chapter, which often hadn't meshed with the main body of The Association of Northwest Steelheaders. We convened a special meeting, disbanded the club, and donated our war chest to the parent organization. It was the right thing to do at the time. The club had become a gathering for socialites where eight people served two hundred members and little else. My feelings always remained mixed but leaned toward complete dam removal. My detractors were fond of reminding me that the dam still stood. To me, the dam became a symbol of my own failure. It had become part of my life's mission, an obsession, and I needed it gone. It was a lesson in frustration, humility, and patience. I had a while longer to wait.

Chapter 10

The Beat Goes On

For death and life, in ceaseless strife, Beat wild on this world's shore,
And all our calm is in that balm Not lost but gone before. — Caroline Norton

Meanwhile, in my personal life, I had been having problems correlating my ever emerging and expanding environmental and political beliefs with my environmentally unfriendly job working for the US Forest Service as a heavy equipment operator, so after six years I quit.

A week later, Leonard (Bub) Berryman and I started a salvage company designed specifically to buy and turn obsolete logging equipment into prepared scrap. Prepared scrap was steel, cut into pieces 18"x18"x60" or less. As all the giant low elevation timber became logged out and unavailable, smaller, higher elevation timber was all that was left for harvest. New machinery had been developed for harvesting timber on steeper slopes. Logging equipment was changing from giant cable machines to smaller, more nimble hydraulic machines. Often, a company would abandon a huge old machine because it was worthless in their eyes and not worth the cost of hauling and storing it somewhere else. As logging companies moved from timber sale to timber sale, they would stash the obsolete machinery on forest service land. A situation developed when the Sierra Club found these obsolete machines offensive and notified the US Department of Agriculture, who ordered their subsidiary the US Forest Service and then notified the logging companies that the machinery had to be removed from public land. Bub and I ran the math on how much money we could make for taking these machines apart on site. Prepared scrap was worth $18 per ton and delivered to the Zidell scrap yard under the Ross Island Bridge in Portland, Oregon. Bottled oxygen and acetylene used to run a cutting torch ran $1.50-$2.00 for the largest bottles. We figured it would cost us $3.00 per ton to process and $3.00 per ton to deliver. That netted us $12.00 per ton to pay our wages. We could haul seven tons legally per trip with my flatbed truck and easily make two daily trips. Each of us would make $10 per hour, a big jump over the $2.25 per hour the Forest Service had been paying me. We got a clear title to 27 pieces of obsolete equipment with no cash expenditure but provided a written guarantee to clean up each site enough to pass government inspection. The smallest piece was rated at 60 tons; the largest was 120 tons. We moved in on the first piece and cut the first load of 7 tons which should have paid $84. The cashier paid me $315 cash. Prepared scrap had jumped to $45 per ton. By the time we were done with the first machine, the price had jumped to $68 per ton, $476 per load. Fuel, oxygen, and acetylene never changed for the duration of the project. We hadn't taken into consideration how many bronze bushings there were in these old machines, which amounted to hundreds of pounds per machine, at $2.30 per pound. From our perspective, we made a killing for two years. My wages had increased by 2600%, and in my mind, I was doing something good for the environment on the planet we all live on.

In 1972, after nine years, my first marriage failed. During the previous year, my wife had become an addict and got involved with some really bad people. She left me with our four children. I thought, "Good riddance!" I hired a babysitter and got on with my life. Three of the children were in school, and the other was in preschool. It wasn't easy, but I, the kids, and the babysitter found a routine. Three months went by. I came home one afternoon and saw that my front door was broken in. The babysitter was lying on the floor unconscious, and my children were gone. My junky wife and her junky boyfriend had taken them.

I phoned the authorities, who were insensitive. Two days later, a letter arrived from the State's

Attorney General demanding child support. I requested access to the children and was informed my estranged wife had filed a restraining order. She falsely claimed that I had beaten her and the children. I paid the child support, hired an attorney, acquired a semiautomatic in a shoulder holster, and went hunting. It took a couple of months, but I found the kids in a bug- infested motel room and took them back. The next six months could fill a whole chapter, but it might not be appropriate here. Suffice it to say, I finally got the junkies out of my life, got full custody of my kids, and settled into single-parent life. I needed a temporary job where I could make a livable wage each day without having any extra responsibility. What I needed was an eight to five job.

I went to work at Zidell Shipyards, dismantling ships under the Ross Island Bridge. This is where we had sold all our logging machinery scrap. Of a long list of dangerous jobs, it was by far the most dangerous. Steamships used crude oil as fuel. Therefore, every steamship was a flammable floating oil tank. Every part of the ship was also coated with flammable paint. Crews would cut the ships apart while they were tied to a sea wall. Giant cranes would lift these sections of ship and set them on dry land where guys like me would turn them into prepared scrap. In the yard, men worked in pairs as teams. The first guy I was paired with was a guy named Big Mike who spent our first hour together telling me how tough he was. It didn't take long for me to notice that Big Mike was hitting a flask every half an hour. By noon I had made up my mind that Big Mike and I were not destined to be workmates. During lunch, I got a new partner. A month later Big Mike dropped a heavy piece of metal on my replacement and killed him.

As a single parent, I allowed myself one evening off each week. The rest of the time, I was a dedicated parent and wage-earner. Even my conservation work took a back seat. No doubt, during this period, I viewed women and children as liabilities. But as a healthy young male, I also desired female companionship, which was often found at the local pubs. One Saturday evening, while sitting at the bar in the Inn Between Tavern, a cute, smiling, curly- headed, buxom young woman took the empty stool beside me. I bought her a drink. Her name was Patty. She was pleasant but appeared too ladylike to be what I was looking for. It was early in the evening, and I moved on to the Barlow Trail Inn, where there was live music. Patty came through the door an hour later, and I asked her to dance. We shut the place down, and I took her home.

It was the next day that I found out she was also a single parent. After about six months, we bought a larger house and combined families. As the years went on, we became aware we had nearly everything in common, such as a love for fly fishing and a lust for adventure. From my end, it was like Patty was always able to anticipate what I needed and show up with it before I even actually realized I desired it. She avoided things that offended me and always made herself extremely convenient. She has always had a very practical, pragmatic way of looking at everything, and after what I had been through, that was very refreshing. For the first time ever, I had a female partner that was solid and dependable. Forty eight years later, we are still together.

Chapter 11

Paying Our Dues

"You got to pay your dues to sing the blues ...

And you know it don't come easy.

--Ringo Starr

Zidell's ship dismantling operation went on strike, and I left them. Patty owned a rental house in Lincoln City, and it needed repair. She and I completely renovated it in the next ten days. It gave me time to think. In the back of my mind, I had thought of having a fly-fishing specialty store. Lack of confidence and other commitments had kept me from doing so. But Patty was encouraging. She said that she would be glad to back the project for an equal partnership in it. After the rental was repaired, I looked around sporting goods stores to see if there were any opportunities for training. I met Larry Schoenborn, the owner of Larry's Sports Center in Gresham, while he was behind his gun counter. He was a short, bright-eyed, athletic, and energetic kind of guy. I explained my work background of years in construction and demolition but admitted that I knew nothing about retail. Then I told him about my experience with hunting and fishing and my

Northwest Steelheaders Organization, etc. I told Larry that I wanted to learn, and I was willing to start at the bottom. He hired me, and ten months later, I was promoted to store manager.

By 1974, bamboo fishing rods had disappeared from the marketplace. Fiberglass rods had replaced bamboo. Fiberglass was more readily available, less expensive, more consistent, more durable and took less maintenance than bamboo. The first graphite fly rods came to market in 1973. They were from the leading fiberglass rod maker, Fenwick. There was so much breakage in the new rushed-to- market rods they broke the company. By the time I left Larry's in 1979, Fenwick was nearly out of business, but graphite from other manufacturers had replaced fiberglass as the most popular rod-building material.

Fly lines had been modernized as well. Before WWII, all fly lines were made from braided oiled silk. They took a lot of care. After the war, fly fishing lines were made of synthetic materials that required very little maintenance and lasted for years. All aspects of fly fishing got easier and more affordable during the 1970s. Fly fishing started to trickle down into the middle class. This move was not favored by the majority of the aristocrats at the time...and some things will never change. That attitude didn't matter at Larry's. We were full service. We sold athletics, skis, and guns, and the tackle department was huge. We even sold bait. The lowest job in the house was cleaning the sand shrimp refrigerator. The newest employee was always given a mop, a broom, a duster, and a wet rag in a bucket of soapy water.

I left my managerial position in 1979 for a partnership in a home construction company. When I entered the partnership, the housing market was a gold mine, and we made a killing for about four months. Then the market crashed into a recession when the Federal Reserve boosted interest rates to curb inflation. Once again, I was out of work. Worse than that, there were no jobs available. For the first time in my life, I couldn't get a job. For a couple of months, I hunted for work, drew unemployment, and spent way too much time feeling sorry for myself. Patty took a job waiting tables, and our savings dwindled.

In my spare time, the kids and I tied flies at our dining room table. Slowly, I started training them to tie commercial flies in volume. After several months we had accumulated enough high-quality flies for a starting inventory for a small fly shop. That was the answer!

I contacted a real estate agent who owned a rundown shack on Hwy 26, the main artery at the time between Portland and Central Oregon and the Deschutes River drainage. It was a tiny building, about eight hundred square feet, and divided into five rooms. It had no heat, no plumbing, and subgrade wiring. But it had highway frontage and a wide shoulder for parking in the front, and it shared a gravel parking lot with a tavern. I made a deal with the owner to rent the building for $35 per month and do the reconstruction to turn the worthless building into a retail space. We signed a five-year contract, then set up a Porta Potty out back. I got my housing construction crew to help with the remodel. We tore off all the old roofing and patched a sizable hole. Then we tore out all the partitions inside and installed 4" x 16" beams in the roof's ridges, turning the building into one "T" shaped vaulted ceilinged room. An antique wood stove was installed in the middle. The ceilings were finished with brocade, and the walls with pastel yellow peg board. With natural red cedar trim, it was the cutest, coziest, and most rustic fly-fishing specialty store ever seen. On April 21, 1981, our family (Patty, I, and six children) started The Fly Fishing Shop. The kids tied flies at a round table. I'm not sure it caught on with the Portland intelligentsia, but while their kids were going to fancy colleges, mine were learning about the free enterprise system from the school of hard knocks.

Looking back after owning the same business for forty years, many things look different now than when we started. Everything looks different when you are blue-collar rather than white-collar. Working with your head doesn't exclude working with your hands. The job still needs to be completed. Growing up on a farm doesn't prepare a person for dealing with city dwellers, except all people like to be treated nicely....just fundamental stuff. I grew up on a farm with a premium trout stream and the total freedom to fish it, but many of our customers grew up in the city with the constraints of having to mount an expedition to go fishing. There are many differences in attitudes. But a work ethic is just that ...if you are not busy making money for the company, you are wasting company time and money. You are either lubrication or sand in the gear train. You are either speeding the company up or slowing it down. Our total till for our first day in business was $142.68. Most people would have looked at it as a failure. Patty and I looked at it as something to build on.

Customers kept inquiring about a fly fishing guide service, and it became apparent that the retail business was going to take longer to build than anticipated. I already had the equipment and lots of experience catching fish. So, in 1981, in order to bolster my income, I became a fly fishing guide on the Sandy, Clackamas, and Deschutes Rivers. (Check out Chapter: 18)

In the retail game, it took a while to figure out that not all fly fishing equipment was well-tested before being offered for sale. In the 1980s, waders created more problems than all other categories put together. Waders are much more durable now than when we started in business. But the reality is there are only two kinds of waders: those that leak and those that are going to leak. During our third year in business, waders became a real nightmare. The company was called James Scott, and they had the first generation of neoprene waders that were unlined and had to be installed on the body like a condom. That should have alerted me to the true nature of the situation. Condoms are only made for one purpose, but in the case of the James Scott waders, it was me, my company and my customers who got screwed. All their waders leaked, and their warranty was fickle as well. So, we lost money and severely damaged our reputation. Following the James Scott fiasco, there was a five-year period when we quit selling waders because no brand was dependable. It took several years for the American wader manufacturer, Simms, to cure the wading gear situation. They set the bar high enough that several brands of dependable waders now exist.

Eventually, we were able to sell more flies than the kids could produce. I had envisioned having all our flies constructed in the local community. We thought it would be the kind of industry that would appeal to single parents or disadvantaged people. After trying to make it happen for a couple of years, we found it not to be so. We finally joined the rest of the fly fishing industry and bought our flies from vendors who sold flies tied in East Asia. My son Troy started a fly tying factory in Mexico. They were beautiful flies of unparalleled craftsmanship and consistency. The 2008 meltdown put an end to that venture.

From the beginning, we put out a lot of printed advertising: sale flyers, magazine ads, brochures, business cards, hatch charts, and fly lists. All that stuff kept our name in front of our customers. Our most ambitious project was the Fly Fishing Wish Book, a pen and ink illustrated black and white catalog featuring my black and white line drawings of products, maps, and fishing scenes. It started as a single page fold over, then became a fourfold brochure, and finally, in 1986, a 12-page catalog. By 1997, The Wish Book had developed into a 70-page edition. For the last five years, we printed and stapled our catalog inhouse, in small batches as needed. By 1995 the same information morphed onto our website. For two years, we had both The Wish Book and our most basic website. In fact, the information flowed from the Wish Book to the website because the print and the line art illustrations were already digitized for the layout of the Wish Book. In 1997 we got a cease and desist letter from a law firm in Chicago advising us to quit using the title "Wish Book." Sears and Roebuck had trademarked the name back at the turn of the century. We could have changed the name of our catalog and continued with it and the website, but I envisioned the web as being the future. From 2001 until 2020, we put out an online newsletter and blog every week. (Check out Chapter: 14)

Sharing a parking lot with a tavern has assets and liabilities. One downside is how much crap goes on next to the wall of your building while you are trying to sleep. An upside in the 1980s, was how many keen anglers you got to party with after you closed the store. A notable evening was the one I got to spend with singer John Denver. I closed the shop, but it was my week to sleep on sight to keep the place from getting broken into. The door of the Inn Between Tavern was thirty feet straight across the lot from our side door, an easy trek. The place was very crowded, with one seat open at the bar. I took the seat, looked over my right shoulder and said, "Hi, John Denver." He was easy to recognize from his record jacket. He and part of his band were fishing with Jim Teeny the next day. John was very enjoyable to be around until the wee hours. I think he had more stamina than I did. I quit and went to bed. Of course, I had to open at 6:00 AM. It was probably a good thing that Jim Teeny usually started fishing at noon. (Check out Chapter: 17)

By 1984 Patty and I had been together for ten years and had never taken a vacation nor had either of us been out of the United States. At that time, our new business was three years old. It was time for an adventure. On advice from a well-traveled fly-fishing friend, Brian O'Keefe, we settled on Placencia, Belize, as a destination. Belize is the only English-speaking country in Central America. The country also has the planet's second longest barrier coral reef and 365 offshore cays. The main draw is the exceptional saltwater flats fishing. After our original five-day fishing trip, we added another ten-day trip, each year, for the next thirteen years. It is fun traveling with Patty, who is short and stocky with a sunny personality, not the archetypal persona of a predator. Most Latin American guides haven't been around many American female fly fishers. Patty is a highly skilled fly angler. We learned to catch bonefish, permit, tarpon, Jacks, snappers, and many other kinds of fish, and we especially enjoyed catching the giant barracudas from the reefs. After fishing with her for a couple of days, one Belize guide nicknamed her Barracuda Patty because of all the Cudas, over thirty pounds, she caught. (Check out chapters: 24-26).

By 1986 we had outgrown our cute little store. It was time to move to a new location.

Chapter 12

A New Beginning

"It is never too late to be what you might have been."

--George Eliot

Part of our business plan was to work steadily to improve fishing while we were in business. It was a good model. By 1986 our business had grown large enough that we needed a larger facility, so we moved uptown to the Hoodland Shopping Center and occupied a 1200- square-foot space in the middle front of the Center.

Many of the people who formerly belonged to The Mt. Hood Chapter of The Association of Northwest Steelheaders had gotten together and formed a looser-knit organization named the Mt. Hood Independent Steelheaders. We worked on local projects in cooperation with the Oregon Department of Fish and Wildlife (ODFW.) From 1979 through the 1980s, we were blessed with record runs of Steelhead throughout the Pacific Northwest region, including the Sandy River Basin. By some counts, possibly exaggerated, the 1979/80 run of winter Steelhead was estimated at 16,000 fish, with another 4,000 Skamania summer Steelhead for a total of 20,000 Steelhead for the year 1980. If you knew a lot about fishing and had your hook in the water, it was hard not to catch a Steelhead that year. ODFW proudly took all the credit, claiming that the big increase was mostly due to their new efficient hatchery programs. We were skeptical. There weren't any regulations to keep sportsmen from killing wild fish. A large percentage of the winter Steelhead that sportsmen were harvesting didn't show any signs of having been in a hatchery.

Rainbow Trout, including Steelhead, inhabit fast-flowing streams where nutrients pass through watersheds quickly. In these watersheds, Rainbow Trout are forced to live in dispersed populations. They are not school fish by nature, and rather, they are singular hunters. Conversely, hatchery-rearing ponds force Rainbow Trout into an overcrowded, unnatural, traumatic lifestyle. This forces each fish to seek open territory by nipping at the fins of the other fish in their living space. Repeated nipping results in fin ray mutilation. Most hatchery Steelhead have un-naturally bent rays in their fins. Once the rays are broken, they are deformed for life. Wild Steelhead grow up in conditions where fin mutilation seldom occurs, and it is easy for an experienced angler to tell the difference in fish resulting from natural or hatchery origin.

The Salmon and Trout Enhancement Program (STEP) was established by the Oregon Legislature in 1981 as a program of the ODFW to allow private parties, under supervision, to do volunteer projects to restore fisheries. The Mt. Hood Independent Steelheaders invested wholeheartedly into the STEP Program. My wife Patty was appointed to the STEP Board of Directors by Oregon Governor Neil Goldschmidt (unfortunately, in later years, he left the governorship in terrible controversy.) Over a period of several years, we worked with several resolute ODFW appointed STEP biologists. A system of twelve hatch boxes was set up on tributary streams and they produced millions of Coho, Steelhead, and Spring Chinook fry each season for ten years. It would be impossible to figure out paybacks, or if there were any.

Our most beneficial project was in cooperation with biologist Wayne Bowers. We fin marked (clipped the adipose fins off) all the hatchery winter Steelhead smolts planted in the Sandy River for three seasons. This project was fraught with challenges. All Sandy River hatchery winter Steelhead smolts were raised at the Gnat Creek Hatchery over 150 miles downriver from Welches. This posed a huge logistical nightmare for us. There was a fully furnished, state-owned, double-wide trailer on the property, but we weren't allowed to use it. We had to carpool for more than three hours of hard driving and then work eight back-breaking hours every day to achieve our goal of fin-clipping 225,000 uncooperative Steelhead pre- smolts, using 7-9 volunteers. The hatchery manager hated the idea of the project and did everything possible to sabotage it, including mixing all our fin-clipped fish with non-fin- clipped fish to kill our first year's work. This angered my buddy Herb to the point that he pulled some strings and got the Gnat Creek Hatchery audited. The audit disclosed that there were large annual discrepancies in equipment bought vs. equipment received over several years. There was an investigation into where the large amounts of money went and who was responsible, and the ODFW personnel at the hatchery was changed. Our next two years of fin clipping went much easier. I believe these projects compelled Oregon to fin-clip all hatchery Steelhead smolts from that point on. When the state of Oregon finally adopted catch-and-release regulations on Steelhead, anglers could easily identify wild fish. If a Steelhead had its adipose fin, it was not legal to harvest.

Another great STEP Program project we worked on with biologist Wayne Bowers was the Adult Sandy River Winter Steelhead Scale Sample

Study. Reading fish scales under magnification is much like reading tree rings. Tree and scale rings can tell you much about the organism that produced them, such as how old they were and how fast they grew. Scales from Steelhead can tell you how many years a fish spent in freshwater and how many years it spent at sea before returning, how many times it returned to spawn again, etc. Scale Sample Gathering Packets were handed out and collected as a program in a partnership between Oxbow Regional Park and The Fly Fishing Shop in Welches, Oregon. Over a full two year study period, 3,500 scale samples were collected from Sandy River winter Steelhead. Five hundred samples were from wild fish. Of the wild fish samples, 21% had not gone to the ocean before the end of their third year. The rest had gone to sea near the end of their second year. Another popular set of projects with Wayne was the Electroshock Stream Surveys. Every tributary in the Upper Sandy River Basin, not on government land, was shocked to stun fish which were gathered for scientific research. We found many small Coho Salmon juveniles, small Cutthroats and Rainbows, and no invasive species. Sometimes it was hard to tell whether we were a bunch of fly fishers that did a lot of fishery improvements or a bunch of stream improvement people that owned a fly fishing shop.

In 1989, the original wooden structure of the Marmot Dam failed. Instead of taking this opportunity to remove the dam, PGE elected to replace it with one built from reinforced concrete. I got a bad case of the blues thinking we had lost that fight and that this new dam would be relicensed and last at least another one hundred years. Seeing twenty years' worth of work gone forever made me hate the world, and I went through a period of doubting everything. For several years, my attitude got worse and worse until I started imagining crosshairs on certain people's foreheads, an unhealthy disposition. I had to distance myself from the world of fishery politics. I did, but I continued to keep one ear to the ground.

Meanwhile, our fly-fishing store prospered. In 1992 the Robert Redford movie: *A River Runs Through It* sparked huge national interest in the sport of fly fishing. The movie story was taken from a book of the same name by Norman Maclean featuring a religious Montana family of fly anglers. The movie got several Oscar nominations, the yuppy crowd ate it up, and many wanted to become fly fishers. It was kind of like the phenomenon of the 1950's when everyone wanted to become a cowboy. Hollywood fuels a huge economic engine. We rode the wave through the 1990s. The Steelhead runs came back in the 2000's and the wave continued.

The newly renovated fish ladder at the Marmot Dam worked very well for the upstream passage of adult fish but was still problematic for downstream passage of both juveniles and adults. Good fish runs continued through the 1980's but the returning numbers of adult fish fell off through the mid-1990s. A few biologists in the ODFW started to side with a couple of fish conservation organizations we had supported. They concluded that the hatchery runs of Steelhead were the cause of the wild fish decline. We thought, "Wow, what if they are right but we continued to support the hatchery program?" In retrospect, it would be hard to prove if the hatchery systems were the main cause of wild fish decline or if natural fluctuations in both freshwater and saltwater survival conditions might have had more influence. The hatchery program, which had been influential in fueling our community tourist business and our retail and guided trip business, came under severe attack and was shut down.

Fortunately, our internet business picked up part of the slack for The Fly Fishing Shop but the tourist business in the surrounding Hoodland community fell on hard times and has never recovered. Because of our sympathy for the wild fish cause, many in the community blamed us for the removal of the hatchery program, so we lost business there too. It is not hard to imagine that perhaps one of the competing, big city, fly shops might have used the hatchery vs. wild issue to damage our business as well.

In spite of the various setbacks our business grew steadily through this period primarily because of our web sales. (These are numbers relative on an annual basis). Let's say the hatchery fishery was worth $1,000 per day ($350,000 annually), and the internet business was worth $1,500 per day ($525,000 annually). Our internet sales growth covered the cost of the fishery loss, but our business was geared toward the $875,000 of the combined sales. We thought our $350,000 fee for creating the community two million dollar cash cow was an equitable return on investment. It was a very popular community asset. We never envisioned anyone would have disagreed with it. But it happened.

Massive state and federal stream improvement projects were introduced to the drainage in the 1990s and continue today. Logging debris used to be burned. Now, much of it is being transferred to our local streambeds. Subgrade logs, stumps, and root wads are built into artificial log jams. There is no doubt that in this era, if you want to catch larger resident trout, they will be found under and around these structures. At first look it seemed to be a win-win for both man and fish. Loggers profited, the community profited, and the fish had more agreeable living space. Why then, after thirty years of such projects, haven't wild Steelhead runs dramatically increased over the normal natural fluctuations?

I have always been a believer that all fish populations are dependent on nurturing habitats. Anything else would seem counterintuitive. Fact is, according to the catch records of my guide service, we had more Steelhead before the hatchery program was emasculated in the 1990s. It would be much to my liking if the habitat improvement worked. It would fit my idea of a perfect world. In this world, it would be much like the early Christian and the Central American Maya culture; man would have dominion to bring order out of chaos. When mistakes were made, human society could fix them. When nature took a turn, not suiting the expectations of society, society could bend nature to its will. The following is an example of why it may not happen easily, or maybe not at all. During the summer of 1996, after ten years of permit applications and design submissions, a quarter mile-long side channel on the Salmon River, the largest Upper Sandy River basin tributary, went through a massive change. The entrance to the channel was altered so it ran water, year around, and was designed with shaded holding pools. Layers of logs were added for fish cover. Most of these structures were anchored to live trees and giant boulders in the streambed. By the end of July, the project was a beautiful monument to modern man's healthy stewardship. Snow came early that year, in huge volume. Then the Pineapple Express came, a climatic condition that happens when the jet stream drops south to the Hawaiian Islands and brings atmospheric rivers of rain to the Pacific Northwest. For three weeks in November 1996, floods peaked three times and were the most devastating floods in the Sandy River drainage since 1964. Roads and houses disappeared, and so did the community's trophy habitat improvement project. Ninety days after careful placement in the rewatered side channel, the logs drifted downriver during the flood. At the mouth of the Sandy, thirty miles downstream where it meets the Columbia, these same logs became part of the refuse that formed log jams against piers supporting the Interstate 84 highway bridge. They were cleared away to protect the bridge and who knows where they ended up after that.

In 2004 in Northern England, at a place named Chesters where there had been a Roman fort and gate on Hadrian's Wall, I was standing on the foundation of a Roman bath house built in 146 A.D. from Vesuvius concrete and squared rock. There had once been a bridge at this spot spanning the Tyne River that eventually enters the English Channel at Newcastle. From my viewpoint there was a long pool with even flow, the kind favored by anadromous fish of many varieties. My eyes are always drawn to water, especially this kind of water. As if by command, a huge colored but clean male Atlantic salmon performed a nose, dorsal, and tail rise right in front of me, showing his prominent adipose fin. Time raced across my mind. Newcastle was a RAF headquarter during World War II, and it had received tons of Nazi bombs during the battle of Briton. Twenty miles south, there is an archaeological excavation of a wooden henge that was built 5,500 years ago. Records show that for the last five thousand years the Tyne River Valley had been under the plow and near constant war, and still there were wild salmon in this river. They could withstand the meddlesome destruction of the human race. It was a revelation, and a heavy weight was gently lifted from my shoulders. If wild Atlantic salmon could survive the onslaught of the human race, Pacific salmon and Steelhead would probably also survive. However, the total numbers of average returns would probably not support or sustain any sports fishery, not even a catch and release one. But at least they might survive until a more enlightened human society took over.

Chapter 13
Hard Work and Persistence Pays Off

"Start by doing what's necessary; then do what's possible, and suddenly you are doing the impossible."

--Francis of Assisi

Ours was one of the first fly fishing specialty stores with a fully functioning website in the mid-1990's. A friend and fellow fly fisher, Steve Kruse, came into the shop and said he had been surfing the internet. I asked, "That's great Steve, what's an internet?" He explained that it was the new world wide web of connected server computers, forming a global cortex. That evening after dinner at his house, he showed Patty and me the internet on his personal computer. Steve's employer, Timberline Lodge, already had a website. The woman who had built it was looking for a larger project to showcase her skills and would work for free. Would I like to be introduced to her? I said, "Yes." Turns out her husband was the real internet expert. She was his apprentice but knew the basics.

We were introduced to the internet in April 1995, and one month later, we were online. After thirty days of her volunteering, I decided we needed a business agreement. We settled on a percentage of the gross with a two-year contract. However, after only a year, she and her husband got into a fight and decided to divorce. She quit our website with a full year left on the contract. My youngest son Derek joined the team, and we adapted Microsoft FrontPage to the existing platform. Derek worked as an adviser and search engine optimization expert. Although my corporate title was CEO, I became a web master of www.FlyFishUSA.com. In 2014 we upgraded to a mobile friendly platform.

In late 1999, we made a deal on a 6,000-square-foot building with frontage on Hwy 26. Part of it had been built in the 1930s as a Post Office with an attached residence. A small grocery store was added in 1962, and it operated as such until the State Highway Department took half of the front parking lot for expansion of Hwy 26. The grocery store had been divided into five smaller rental units. Once again, I contacted my crew from the home-building days, and we got to work starting with tearing out the partitions. The building had been constructed with posts supporting huge, natural wood glue-lam beams, and a matching ceiling fourteen feet from the floor. In the 1960s, wood was inexpensive. In the 2000s, this kind of wood had become rare and unaffordable. Patty did a masterful job of renovating the ceiling and beams, giving the three thousand square foot showroom a rich, warm, and expansive personality. What had been a grocery store, post office, and residence became the ultimate fly fishing specialty store for the modern age. The architecture was "wild-western" with a huge showroom, modern classroom, offices, shipping center, photo and art center, and ample warehouse. We were located in the Upper Sandy River basin, with proximity to year-round Steelhead and salmon fishing in every direction, and it was all combined with an innovative web site drawing world trade.

I was standing on a ladder in the middle of the store while the remodel crew was busily working on the same room when the phone rang. Patty answered it, and I heard her say, "I don't know, let me get him." She handed me the phone. It was Fred Evans, a popular personality on a hyperactive web discussion group called "Spey Pages." Fred needed no introduction to me. I had followed his threads for a couple of years. He said, "There are a bunch of guys getting together at Oxbow Park on the Sandy River and they are planning a Spey Clave next May. Would the shop be interested in participating?"

"What is a Clave?" I asked.

Fred explained, "Clave, you know, short for Conclave, a gathering." He explained that it would be a gathering of anglers on the river to explore the dynamics of Spey tackle and Spey casting. Could we provide some tackle to try and instructional assistance?

In this context, the word "Spey" means a type of casting and fishing with two-hand fly rods that seems to have evolved on Scotland's Spey River in the 1800s. Although the technique was known to many American anglers, it had never become popular in the United States until the publication of Steelhead Fly Fishing, written by Trey Combs in 1990. Trey highlighted several successful Steelhead anglers' fishing rivers in Northern Washington State and British Columbia. They had found success fishing both summer and winter Steelhead using Spey-style equipment. The paradigm shifted quickly. Within a year, it seemed everyone wanted to know about catching Steelhead with this method which had been traditional Atlantic salmon tackle in Europe for over two hundred years. My own experience with fly fishing for Steelhead started in the mid-1960s, and our store featured Steelhead fly fishing schools and guided trips. We had been deep into the Pacific Northwest Spey Revolution since before 1990. The idea of a public Spey Fishing program on our home water had appeal. I explained to Fred that we were in the middle of a business expansion but that I would think it over and call him back within sixty days. The new store projects went smoother than anticipated and were finished on time and slightly under budget.

In the meantime, I talked to four different

tackle reps that were committed to supplying the tackle. The first Sandy River Spey Clave didn't have much structure and only drew about fifty people, but everyone really enjoyed it. The original organizers had chosen the perfect site, Group Area "Alder" at Oxbow Park. It had a covered pavilion for displays and was situated on a long straight pool with a sandbar that made it perfect for a large crowd to watch demonstrations or try out tackle.

At the end of the program, someone asked if there would be another next year. A voice in the crowd said, "Bachmann, you ought to take this thing over and do it right." There was an immediate cheer. I thanked them for their confidence and agreed to organize the next Sandy River Spey Clave. Patty and I agreed that the site at Oxbow Park was the best in Oregon for such an event, but it was a long way from town, and we would have to feed people to hold a crowd. She organized a kitchen group from the local women's' fly fishing clubs for the first year. Over the years, many different groups helped with breakfasts, lunches, and dinners. Patty's chocolate chip cookies were a huge hit. She baked an average of 3,000 cookies per Clave for 19 Claves, 57,000 cookies in total! We turned the event into a two-day affair, giving people a reason to attend from out of state. Many folks stayed in the campground in the park, and for the first time ever, it was full. Many other people stayed in local motels in Portland, Troutdale, and Sandy.

The first tackle rep who signed up with the Sandy River Spey Clave was Randy Sholes, who at the time was working for Cortland Line Company. Cortland had just signed a deal to be the United States importer and distributor for the English fly tackle manufacturer Hardy Randy advised me that Hardy's vice president of foreign sales, Andy Murray, would be available to do an on-the- water presentation about Spey casting. As soon as the word got out that Andy was going to be at the Clave, it was easy to get many of the other "big guns" involved. With help from all the major fly tackle rep groups, we turned the Sandy River Spey Clave into the largest free Spey College on the planet. The Sandy River Spey Clave became the epicenter of the Spey Revolution.

Key to the event were a dozen on-the-water programs with leading Spey celebrities such as Simon Gawesworth, Al Bhur, and George Cook, just to name a few. Some of the local female anglers asked if they could do a "women's day." We added a third day, featuring women for several years, then integrated the ladies into our regular program with the guys.

The Sandy River Spey Clave became the

preeminent program of its kind in the world and lasted until 2019 until the Covid epidemic put it out of business. It peaked in 2014 when 16 rep groups brought Spey tackle to nearly two thousand attendees. This program became the blueprint for many other such events around the country, but none ever attained the same prestige or attendance.

Through our association with Cortland and Hardy, Andy Murray became an instructor in several of our Deschutes River Summer Steelhead PhD Spey Schools from 2002 - 2004. In November 2004, Patty and I were invited to visit the Hardy factory and headquarters. We stayed in England/ Scotland for a ten day period. Two things became evident to us about the British Isles: if the land isn't paved, there are sheep on it and, nice people wear wool.

On the British Isles they have been stacking rocks for a very long time and some new construction is similar to buildings made hundreds of years ago. Our main residence was a coaching inn built in 1670 in the town of Wooler in Northumberland just south of the Scottish border. From Wooler we ranged into Scotland as far north as Grantown-on-Spey and spent the night there. Coming back south in the Spey River Valley, I noted that the fuel gauge in our vehicle registered only a quarter of a tank and I pulled into a little town called Aviemore for gas. While I pondered the self-service pumps, a jet black BMW pulled into the opposite lane. A slick looking, middle-aged man wearing a wool tweed suit got out of his car, removed the filler cap, and stuck the pump nozzle in his auto, then he eyed me with suspicion. I was dressed in blue jeans and a red and black, plaid, fleece shirt that looked like wool. With a heavy brogue he asked tersely, “Is that the plaid of the Black Stuarts?” I replied that I knew plaids were emblems of clan affiliation, but I was from the USA and wished not to offend anyone. His attitude changed and he asked what part of the USA? My reply was, “Oregon.” He asked what part of Oregon and I replied, “a place no one in Scotland had probably ever heard of called Welches.” His next statement stunned me, “You know, they have a great fly shop in Welches, Oregon?” My reply was, “Yes, I own that fly shop.” His answer stunned me again, “Then you must be Mark Bachmann,” and he stuck out his hand. I shook his hand and admitted it was true. Then I queried, “How could you know that? We are eight thousand miles from home and don’t know anyone in this town.” The man introduced himself and said he was a doctor. He informed me his son was studying to be a doctor and while taking classes at OHSU in Portland, Oregon he had decided to fish the Deschutes River. He stopped at The Fly Fishing Shop in Welches and was treated well. He had since moved to Phoenix, Arizona for further schooling and had dealt with us online and had recommended that his father should do the same. The father had recognized me from pictures on our website. It truly is a small world.

Most things worked to our advantage through the early 2000s. Columbia River Steelhead runs were the largest ever recorded from 2001 until 2014. Then they began to fall off. Our web presence became dominant in the industry. We owned all the best fly-fishing search terms on Google, and we got orders from all over the world. The UK, Scandinavia, Mainland Europe, Australia, and Japan were especially good customers. The business that started on our dining room table, with kids tying flies, was now bringing in a couple of million dollars per year. We were taking a foreign destination fly fishing trip each quarter, which gave us an unprecedented amount of expertise and prestige. We packed our fly gear and visited other states like Montana, Florida, Texas, and other countries such as Russia, Mexico, Belize, Bahamas, and the UK. We were in the first fly fishing group to visit Cuba through their front door. We were paying our bills on time, and manufacturers were giving us special deals. It was a great life! Unfortunately, though, it was the calm before the storm.

By 2006 our new nifty website had grown to nearly two thousand pages and to three thousand by 2008. But we were having problems getting products on time and therefore having problems delivering products to our customers in a timely manner. There were many lost opportunities because there were no employees adaptable enough for the new technologies. There was too much bickering and poor performance among the newly expanded crew of employees. Just hiring people who had a work ethic became an unsolvable problem. We were drowning in paperwork and overhead brought on by the complexity of the larger business, more moving parts, more taxes, and regulations. The marketplace was chaotic and unpredictable. The whole industry seemed undercapitalized and held together by Band-Aids. Our prized anadromous fishery was shriveling. Patty saw it coming before I did. She said the supply of fly fishing tackle is expanding faster than the demand. She was filling out the forms, paying the bills, and checking in the stock. She was closer to the money stream, which is where the bottom line is to be found in doing business. You are either making a profit or not. In retail, you are either selling as many products as you are buying or not. To be a sustainable business, it has to generate a positive cash flow which was becoming more difficult. Success is more about markups and turns than displaying the latest model. Actually, it is about both.

Even before the crash came, there were termers in the Force. Fly fishing as a sport was losing its traction. Its aristocratic attitude hadn't caught on with the masses. It has never dawned on many aristocrats that not everyone wants to be one of them. The expansion of the fisheries through the seventies and eighties were ended by the wild fish only movements of the nineties and two-thousands. The leaders in that group were mostly fly fishers and wanna-be aristocrats. Most fly fishers were categorized as being part of that group. The wild fish only group was proud of their work and were more than happy to take the blame. It is probably only coincidence a massive drop in returning Steelhead and Chinook salmon followed a few years after the first decade of the two thousand. We will probably never know the real facts as to why that happened.

The manufacturing part of the industry wanted larger profits but realized the market was controlled by the amount of fishing opportunities available. They saw no room for expansion there. So, they shortened the length of their production runs from ten years to seven years, then to four years. In the auto industry, this approach is called built in obsolescence. This era did result in some notable innovations but also in a lot of copycat junk, some of it very expensive, and some of it unreliable, expensive junk. This overproduction caused inflation by devaluing products and the sport as a whole in the marketplace. There is nothing more obsolete than a previous model fly line because the newest really is always the best. In this category, "Made in the USA" really does mean something. Yet some anglers will fish with an old beat-up fly line for years after it should have landed in a campfire. They were probably the kids who were dragging around the same worn out teddy bear when they were six. Many would-be anglers are more collectors than fishermen. They buy tackle at bargain prices just to feel good. A lot of closets were over-filled with unused fly fishing junk. Online auction sites such as ebey.com made all of this obsolete tackle viable merchandise to sell online. The result created a parallel economy to the established market plan. A surge in internet sales of every description flooded the marketplace everywhere, especially everywhere most established retailers could not compete. We managed to gain market share despite the distractions…at least for a while.

Chapter 14

Up Then Upside Down

"It is during our darkest moments that we must focus to see the light."

--Aristotle

During a Fly-Fishing Shop weekend fly-tying party in 2000, a regular member of the fly-tying group, and retired BPA executive, Jim Jones, told me he had some inside information. PGE was going to relinquish the license to Marmot Dam. He told me that our battle with the Marmot Dam had been won. He advised me to leave the situation alone and celebrate the victory quietly. I didn't know whether to believe it or not.

Seven years later, on July 24, 2007, I was sitting in a covered waterfront pavilion overlooking Marmot Dam on the Sandy River. PGE had invited each of the one hundred people in the crowd. It was a celebration of the imminent destruction of the dam, a scene envisioned in the winter of 1969. It was finally here in real time. I studied the faces of the other guests but kept to myself and tried to figure out what was going on in the various minds around me. Some faces were new to me, but many were familiar. Many had crossed my path regularly over the last 38 years. Some had been continual naysayers, telling me repeatedly the dam would never be removed. Now they were taking credit for making it happen to further their political careers. I watched and listened in amazement without saying a word. What did it matter who got the credit? Herb too, sitting quietly and calmly, gave me a wink. We knew the truth. Who cares if your battles get grafted into another's legacy? Who cares if want-to-be leaders are only copy-cat followers? A few minutes later, PGE CEO Peggy Fowler pushed the T-handle down on the ignition Dynamo and blew off the top layer of the dam. Three giant track-driven back-hoes started pulling the dam apart before the smoke even settled. Over the next three months, the dam was systematically dismantled. In October, an unseasonable storm brought the Sandy River to flood stage, and it devoured any evidence of the dam ever having been there. Right up until the end there had been a big controversy among stakeholders about whether removal of the dam would create problems for the river environment when all the gravel which had collected behind the dam slumped after the dam was removed. After the first flood receded, it was hard to find where this gravel had been or where it had gone to. The removal of Marmot Dam was a complete success and as such it smoothed the way for the removal of the Powerdale

Dam on the Hood River, the Condit Dam on the White Salmon River and the two high dams on the Elwha River. Suddenly removing dams from rivers in the Pacific Northwest became a thing to do. It was now a politically safe idea and pretty people could back it.

Two-thirds of the way through 2008, everything fell apart. A housing finance bubble crashed the economy. By the end of the first quarter of 2009, we had lost 40% of our business (our last and best five years of growth), and we were in financial free fall. We were scaling back all our programs to cut costs while trying to maintain cash flow. Our main fight was to forestall bankruptcy. The effects of all the reductions in fishery were cumulative, with a negative effect on the tourist industry of the Pacific Northwest. In 2015, the Columbia River Steelhead runs crashed and have remained in a downward trend through 2023. Covid-19 killed off the rest of travel and put a tight cap on public gatherings. At the same time, Metro, the outfit that manages Oxbow Park, tripled permit fees. There was no way we could afford it. The Sandy River Spey Clave died. One by one, our revenue producers shriveled. From a high of over $2 million in 2008, our gross revenue shrank to $335,000 in 2021.

It is much easier to manage a business for

growth than for decline. Patty had always taken responsibility for keeping the books and paying the bills. She had a sophisticated digital bookkeeping system and a one or two-person staff to get the job done, which was challenging when things were good. But it was far more complicated as the business was falling apart. Patty did a masterful job of keeping vendors happy during our 13-year adjustment period. Customers got service, and vendors got paid with interest.

By 2022 we had stabilized our faltering private economy enough to sell off the company in pieces and pay off all our bills. Every creditor got paid in full. As Tyrion Lannister, from the TV epic *Game of Thrones*, was fond of saying, "A Lannister always pays his debts." And so did the owners of The Fly Fishing Shop in the Upper Sandy River Basin in Welches, Oregon!

This book covers 623 years of the human condition and 78 years of my personal history (both with a lot left out). Sixty eight of those years I have been a fly fisher, 54 years an environmentalist and fishery advocate, 42 years a fly fishing guide, 40 years a fly tackle retailer, and for 38 years, a writer. It all continues to be a grand adventure.

In my 54 years as an environmentalist and fishery advocate, I have been very willing to sacrifice the economic assets of others: industrial polluters, dam builders, loggers, river channelizers, commercial fishermen both red and white skinned, catch and kill anglers, open ground agriculturist, irrigators, urban sprawlers, and many, many more who are enemies of the fisheries I love. We all are willing to fight or bargain for what we perceive as a better position for ourselves and our children. I've been perceived as a ruthless, combative, tricky, and sometimes underhanded competitor as an environmentalist, fishing guide, and business owner. If so, I make no apologies or excuses, and it was all premeditated. I knew in the end, there are no winners or losers. We are all leaving this existence with the same amount we came in with. And we are all trying to avoid situations like some of our ancestors who might have had to sell their own children into slavery to avoid starvation or becoming slaves themselves. In the most civilized of situations, there are still freedoms worth killing and dying for.

Decisions are easiest when the results of our work or combat can be clearly viewed. A creek is more than a ditch. A beaver pond is more than a reservoir. Wetlands are signs of stored nutrients in a healthy high water table. All watersheds are best for fish if they are left entirely natural. Some anglers maintain that only wild fish are worth saving. After looking at all the scientific evidence and listening to advocate testimony in an unbiased stance for a time that has been over half of my long life, it is hard to see a clear end to the controversy.

A case in point…a City of Portland fishery biologist asked for my advice. The city had given him partial control of ninety million dollars as mitigation for their destruction of the Bull Run River watershed as Portland's main water source. The river is a tributary of the Sandy River and comprised one-third to one-half the normal flow of the lower Sandy before the dams were built. I worked inside the Bull Run Reserve when working for the Mount Hood National Forest in the 1970s. Below the dams, the Bull Run was a bed rock river like the North Umpqua and still had a vestigial run of native summer Steelhead. From my point of view, there is no amount of mitigation money that can compensate for this kind of loss. There were three options for a solution. One would be to tear out the dams and wait a thousand years for everything to heal and for the native Steelhead to regain their status in the watershed. It is unlikely that even the wild fish advocates who live in Portland were going to agree to that. The second choice would be to swallow the guilt and ignore the situation, which is a more standard procedure in our proud, entitled society. The final option would be to plant hatchery summer Steelhead in other tributaries of the Sandy to become an economic boost to the community. That was the chosen option of the managers in the mid nineteen seventies, year round Steelhead runs. By 2000, hatchery Steelhead had become persona non grata. The Steelhead runs in the Sandy and Clackamas Rivers went from year round to two and a half months. The economic impact is clear in every section of society, but most evident in Estacada on the Clackamas, and Welches on the Sandy. Instead of being tourist resort towns, it turned them into bedroom community towns for Portland.

I told the biologist that if rebuilding wild runs was his goal, then buying and burning waterfront homes would be the best place to put the money. He was shocked and said that Clackamas County would never go along with that plan because they would lose too much from their tax rolls. That might be true, but wild fish require a wild habitat. Dumping logs in a river for habitat restoration is probably a plus but may be much like putting a Band-Aid on a bleeding major artery, you might slow the blood loss, but the patient is still going to bleed to death.

The loss of the hatchery Steelhead runs, with little recovery of the wild fishery, was a major blow to our business. So, we lost, and the other side won. It was just a judgment call, and you never know if something is going to work unless you try. It is probably not the final chapter.

It took 38 years to get the Marmot Dam removed from the Sandy River. It was a grand adventure filled with heroes, villains and even damsels in distress. But don't worry, you didn't miss the boat. There is still plenty left to be done by you and other smart people! And if people want it as a common goal, rivers will become healthy with beautiful wild fish.

In the meantime, you might go fly fishing and experience nature as it is or envision how it was or could be. Or you might look back and be satisfied with your own migratory swim upstream against a turbulent flow. It couldn't have been without mistakes. You just did the best you could. It might be enough to know you were in the thick of it. And you might be lucky like I was yesterday morning with the sun breaking over the east rim. After fishing the Gauge Hole, the best, I could and pulling out too soon, I ran my boat over the sweet spot, and a big steelhead bolted ten casts downstream from where I had quit. Then, after I ran the Mine Field and all the tricky water perfectly into the Blue Hole, my mental and muscular tension disappeared, my lungs deflated, and the sun lit the whole panorama completely…how was I lucky enough to land here in this "Eden-like" scene and in that moment? Because I wanted it that way!

Chapter 15

Redside

"Never let the fear of striking out keep you from playing the game."

--Babe Ruth

Near the edge of a large back eddy, in the shade of streamside alders, I watch the Deschutes River. Upstream, a short riffle ends where the river slows over rough cobble. Ten feet from the near shore, the current breaks around a large boulder that morphs into a slick overhung by brush and tall canary grass protruding from a high bank, cover for a trout and a handicap for right-handed anglers like me.

It's a prime holding spot. The fish rests on the edge of a calm behind the large, flat, angular, mid-stream boulder. Deschutes jade-green water rushes past, toward the Columbia, to end finally in the Pacific. The big trout rests in its lair behind the boulder, nearly invisible, shielded by a curtain of bubbles. In the suction behind the boulder, a tiny eddy traps food and pulls it deeper into the water. The fish has perfect escape routes to either side, into rushing water that will instantly hurtle him away from danger. Long filaments of blue-green algae wave in the flow, further concealing the trout's home. The chunk of basalt, recently discharged from the rimrocks, anchors the filaments and breaks the flow into a cascade that plunges oxygen-laden, silvery-green bubbles deep into the river. They mix with the long trailing algae and bounce off the gravel bed like an endless procession of transparent rubber balls.

The afternoon sun filters through the leaves of the streamside alders. A gentle breeze animates the leaves, changing the spaces between them, turning the rays into dancing columns that penetrate the turbulent surface of the river and play upon the ever-changing pattern of the bubbles. Some of these tiny orbs of light cling momentarily to the algae and other water plants before wandering downstream and back to the surface from whence they came. The water is a melody played by the afternoon sun upon the bubbles full of light.

The current slows next to the bank nearest to the sun. Here the large, smooth, current- swept stones gradually give way to a bottom of sand and silt as the flows diminish. The finer silt provides a solid footing for Elodia plants and all the creatures that live in them. The strands of bright green vegetation trail in the gentle current like an undulating wall of Christmas tree garlands. These fronds are lighter than water. They rise to the surface as the changing currents subside but sink beneath the weight of stronger flows, so they dance up and down, in and out. Their pulse adds melody to the harmony of the bubbles. The Elodia raises on straight stalks and fans out to cover more of the surface of the river than the bottom. It forms caves and funnels and tunnels. Several small trout flit about in the caves under the Elodia, capturing prey as they are washed from the foliage. The big trout needn't waste energy by flitting among foliage in search of prey. The river brings him an endless smorgasbord and deposits them in the tiny eddy inches in front of his pointed snout.

I quietly peek over the streamside vegetation. Several small trout are visible along the edge of the weed bed. One is directly below me. It rises, splashing to the surface and dispatches a small yellow mayfly. My binoculars disclose other mayflies upon the riffle but no other trout rising to them. The rest of the riffle seems barren of fish. My view rests momentarily on the slick behind the boulder. The visibility is unusually good, but the seamy, boiling surface is hard to penetrate. Yet there is a grayish-red cast to the streambed in the far edge of the slick. At first, I think it is a fish. Then I am uncertain. The image seems too large and immobile.

A tiny mayfly nymph leaves the gravel upstream from the boulder. As it struggles to the surface the pressure within its body splits the exoskeleton from the top of its head to the center of its back. A viscous, bleached version of the adult insect emerges through the rent in the skin. First the crumpled wings appear and then the back of the head and finally the thorax, head, and legs. Last to leave the nymphal shuck is the abdomen. Finally, the mayfly rides the choppy, undulating meniscus as a fully developed air-breathing adult. It rides the surface only a short distance and is pulled under by the spill behind the boulder. It pauses, struggling briefly near the bottom. There is a short, swift movement as the trout lunges forward, and the mayfly disappears into the giant maw. At that moment, the fish is fully visible.

Brush and tall weeds surround me. The alders, which shaded me earlier, are now an obstruction to my back-cast. The only possible trajectory for my fly line must be high and behind the trees. The forward cast must change direction to align itself with the target. Since line and fly will land in water travelling at drastically different speeds, there will have to be a lot of slack in the leader to allow the fly to drift naturally. Realizing that the fish will probably become aware after the first shot, my confidence falters as I trace and retrace the path my cast must follow. A brief search for alternatives convinces me there are none.

I inspect the leader and replace the 6X tippet

with three feet of 5X and knot a size #16 low floating yellow mayfly dun tied with legs, tails, and upright Fly-Film wings. The colors, size, and shape match the mayflies hatching from the river. The fly is left undressed to sink quickly beneath the spill below the rock. The leader and twenty feet of fly line hang coiled from my left hand. I raise the rod quickly with my right, and the coils feed out of my other hand into a high back cast that hangs momentarily over the alders. The cast ends in a shallow arc and the forward loop sails out high over the water. The rod tip comes to a stop and the loop changes from vertical to horizontal. An instant before the loop flows into the leader, I push a tiny amount of slack into the line and the cast dies in the air. The fly line lands on the water upstream from the fish, leader pointed downstream, and the fly is on a direct course to the center of the boil below the rock. There is a quick release of air from my lungs and tension from executing the cast is gone.

The fly drifts a foot, and it disappears in the spill. A sudden movement in the slick below the rock makes me raise the rod by reflex more than intent. The line comes instantly tight as water explodes, and a broad caudal fin hurls the fish into the raging current. Trout and fly line blur as white Dacron backing leaves my shrieking reel. The trout launches itself into the air again near the far shore and races downstream into the eddy. A black felt-marker stripe signals that fifty yards of backing have left the reel. Incredibly, the fine leader holds against the pressure of my light rod and the reel's smooth drag. The trout pauses, then runs toward me, and I reel frantically to maintain tension on the line, hoping the tiny barbless hook will stay embedded. The trout shakes its head violently, and I ease off on the pressure as the trout reverses course and the reel spool, smaller in diameter from loss of line, spins its shiny black handle into a blur. A red felt marker stripe signals the reel is almost empty.

Again, the trout pauses. There is no accounting for the luck. A few more yards and I will be out of line, and the light tippet will break. I must follow. Immediately downstream, alders overhanging the deep eddy block my path. The river bottom is mud and sticks. I toss my vest and binoculars into the grass and can barely feel the trout as I slide down the bank into the water. In the river up to my shirt pockets, I fight my way through a raft of flotsam and midge shucks that adhere to my shirt and chest hair. Reeling myself down to the fish, I gain some line. The alder branches hang nearly in the water as I fight my way through underneath them. My feet sink into the bottom before I finally emerge downstream of the alders in a muddy plume. I crawl up the bank, still maintaining pressure and gaining line, but the fish is still far below me as the red marker stripe comes back onto the reel. For a while, the fish gives ground, and I reel continuously until the black stripe is also back on the reel. I am downstream fifty yards below the riffle. Finally, as the backing knot comes into the rod guides, I see my fish, a silvery- green blur deep in the clear water of the eddy. My heart races—a trout larger than I thought! For a long time, the fish stays deep along the far shore and bullies my light tackle with the forceful aid of the midstream current. The backing knot seesaws back and forth through the guides and the line bows downstream as the fish stays directly across the wide green river. At last, constant pressure takes its toll and the big trout gives ground. A few more minutes bring him to hand.

He is wondrous, subdued but still full of life, a male twenty-plus inches in length and nearly five pounds, his body deeper than my hand is long. I can barely close my fingers around the wrist of his tail as I slide him into shallow water. His black-spotted, olive-colored back blends with the skimpy aquatic vegetation and sand. The rose-colored gill plates pump rhythmically. His snout is long and pointed, but the lower jaw lacks the kype of sexual maturity. All his fins are perfect. He has never spawned. The distinctive red stripe from which his species gets its name identifies him as a male and is but a faint glow of the ruby it will become; his pectoral fins sport the same red tinge. All his lower fins are tipped with milky white. His lower sides are silverish amber. Every scale contains a sparkling mirror crescent. His muscles are hard to the touch. Energy returns to his body as he starts to struggle, feeble at first, then with vigor. Complete equilibrium returns slowly. He is tired. I am tired but relaxed as I turn him toward the river, and he struggles free from my hand, his form dissolving into the green depths of the eddy. He is free again, and so am I.

Chapter 16

Jenny

"Love the life you live. Live the life you love."

--Bob Marley

If guiding fly fishermen for forty years has taught me anything it's that fish are great equalizers. Fish don't know how rich, famous, or how skilled you are at bending others to your will. It doesn't matter if you're an expert caster with years of experience, or a rank beginner, how old, young, or what sex you are. Two sayings come to mind: "experience is the best teacher," and "beginner's luck." Often the two seem at odds, but they really aren't. Wealth may purchase you more experience and the leisure to pursue your passions and increase odds in your favor, but luck is essential for expert and beginner alike, and luck, or its lack, visits both. This story is about one of those beginners.

Jenny called me from Chicago about mid-May 1988. Her daughter was staying for the summer near Welches, Oregon and working at one of the ski resorts on Mt. Hood. In September, Jenny was coming to Oregon for a visit and had always wanted to catch a big salmon. It had been her fantasy since she was a girl and had watched a man catch one on the American Sportsman TV show. Her daughter had told her there were lots of big salmon in the Sandy River and had asked locals to recommend a fishing guide. My name kept coming up.

When I asked about her background and game plan, Jenny indicated that she didn't like boats, didn't have much money, and could only afford to pay for four hours of guiding. I asked if she could hike and wade rivers. "Probably not," she answered. She had fibromyalgia, a nervous system disorder that made her weak and impaired her balance. She was a retired elementary school teacher from the inner city.

I asked how much fishing experience she had, and she replied that she had "fished a couple of times for catfish." All my red lights came on. Here was the making of an impossible client, an out-of-shape, middle-aged city woman with high expectations, no skills or experience, and a disease that affects her motor skills and mind. Add to that a tremendous amount of liability exposure. I immediately tried to back out of the situation.

I emphasized I was a fly-fishing guide, and all the equipment I owned was for fly fishing, most of the fish in our rivers were steelhead, and like salmon, were difficult to catch-- especially for a novice. I told her catching a salmon might take more than four hours, even for a highly skilled angler, but I stopped short of saying it was impossible. I told her learning to cast with a fly rod might take more than four hours by itself. She agreed fly fishing was probably out of the picture. She would use her own spinning rod. I pleaded that it had been years since I'd used spinning tackle, but she pleasantly insisted I would probably remember how. This part of our conversation went on for several minutes with me getting firmer and firmer.

Finally, desperate, she said, "This disease is going to kill me! Before that happens, I will be bedridden and finally lose all ability to move. My time is short. I want to catch a salmon! You are my best chance. Are you going to help me or not?"

Who could refuse that? I couldn't. We agreed on a meeting time and place five months into the future. At least that gave me enough time to prepare mentally.

Habitually I review my entire guide calendar every Sunday. Each time September came up, there was Jenny's name on the dreaded 13th. How stupid and weak I had been caving into a task doomed to disappointment, allowing myself to be put on a pedestal I didn't deserve, with no chance of living up to a set of impossible expectations.

Around the first of September, however, my attitude began to change. I'd accepted this job, and it had to be done to the best of my ability. There was no backing out. I reviewed the river in my mind, searching for a place with every advantage before settling for a pool on private property rarely visited. I called my friend Skip who owned the land bordering the pool and explained my situation. Skip is a child psychologist by trade. He immediately sized up my dilemma and advised me on the easiest terrain to follow and latest fishing information.

A week before the trip, I drove to the site and surveyed it in detail. Skip's front yard was nearly all floodplain that sloped gently to the river. There were a few scraggly trees, but little grass or brush, and access to two pools, both good for Chinooks and steelhead. The upper pool was 200 yards from Skip's house. The lower was in front of the house, a shorter walk, but the terrain was more difficult. I walked the trail to the upper pool. The first fifty yards were level and flat. The second one hundred and fifty yards were cut up with old flood channels, which alternated from sand to larger boulders. All in all, it was easy going for a person with normal physical fitness, but I wasn't sure how Jenny might fare.

The upper pool was formed on a sharp turn where the water ran into a high bank on the opposite side of the river. It was deep at the head and remained moderately deep until it tailed out 75 yards downstream. Large boulders littered the bottom of the pool, a perfect fish-holding spot. Between the two pools lay a short but steep boulder-strewn rapid. Along the near side of the rapid a clump of alders had been severely gnarled and undermined by last winter's flood. A couple of broken trunks faced upstream and jutted a couple of yards over the water. The shattered spear points of wood presented a hazard for any angler wading downstream chasing a fish. I looked for a path behind them and found none but managed to wade around in front of them waist-deep on my way downstream to examine the lower pool. The lower pool was narrow and fast where rapids flowed into it. Then it gradually widened, and the water slowed to perfect fish-holding speed for 200 yards. All in all, the terrain looked easy enough to traverse for a person with a modicum of physical strength.

I went home and sorted through a coffee can of fishing junk that had been gleaned from riverbanks over the past few years, mostly an assortment of lures lost by other fishermen. I selected a dozen weighted spinners and a few wobblers that might attract a salmon or steelhead during the current water conditions. Since fishing these lures takes a certain amount of skill my new client probably didn't have, I figured a few would end on the bottom and be reclaimed by the river. Easy come, easy go.

September 13 dawned clear and calm. Jenny and I were to meet at the fly-fishing shop around one o'clock in the afternoon. I kept busy with bookwork through the morning, my exterior calm and confident. But inside was a shadow of foreboding. Jenny came through the door right on time. She wore a wide-brimmed hat and a large smile. Her fragile but friendly demeanor made her attractive. In her right hand was a lightweight spinning rod and reel appropriate for trout rather than salmon or steelhead. I checked the reel. It appeared to be loaded with brand new 8-pound test green monofilament. Jenny wore a wide canvas belt around her narrow waist with a brand-new folding wading staff in a leather sheath. She said her daughter had recently purchased the Fol-Staff and sent it to her as a gift for her Oregon fishing trip. She was wearing shorts and tennis shoes instead of waders.

"How was your flight?" I asked.

"Bumpy." She replied. "My daughter picked me up at

the airport. We had lunch, and she dropped me off here."

"Are you ready to go then?" "Yup! Let's go get

‘em!”

I took her rod and small bag of gear and put them in the back of my Ford van, then quickly came around to the passenger door. She needed my help climbing up into the seat. She was weaker than I had thought and barely had strength enough to stand upright. On our way to the river Jenny explained that exercise for normal people caused muscles to tear, but they healed during sleeping hours. Fibromyalgia didn’t allow you to sleep, so torn muscles never healed, resulting in unbearable pain. “I’ll pay dearly for this adventure,” she said. “But I think it’s worth it.”

No one was home when we got to Skip’s place. It took a couple of minutes for me to put on my chest-high waders. The 200-yard walk to the upper pool, which would have taken a healthy person only a few minutes, turned out to be a challenge for Jenny. Even smaller river rocks were difficult for her. I put a hand in each of her armpits nearly carrying her across a gravel bar. After what seemed like a long time we arrived at water’s edge and Jenny stood, half exhausted, on a small, level sandbar. Several minutes more passed while she regained her strength.

I took her rod and dug around in a small plastic box containing the secondhand lures I’d reclaimed from the river and selected a small, weighted trout spinner with a gold blade, fluorescent, black-dotted orange body, and a tiny size-12 treble hook.

After I had fastened it to the end of her line, I told her to cast it to the center of the river directly in front of us. She swung the rod back but released the line too soon, firing the lure in a high trajectory that veered far left upstream 40 feet from the target. The water looked far too shallow to hold fish. Trying to keep my voice calm I told her to reel quickly before the lure snagged on the river bottom. She cranked the handle in a blur and the line came tight. I assumed the lure was stuck between rocks on the bottom of the river and told her to give the rod tip a hard jerk to free it. What happened next had to be divine intervention or plain old beginner's luck. A huge, male fall Chinook bolted through the surface of the water, the tiny spinner sparkling from its lower jaw. The fish was slightly bronze colored, but clean and fresh looking. It ran upstream the length of the pool and sulked under a sheet of fast-moving water.

Jenny giggled, "Well that wasn't so hard, was it? My daughter said you're the world's best fishing guide. "I smiled back and winked but kept my mouth shut, knowing whatever skills I have had absolutely nothing to do with that fish being hooked—and on a first cast! I checked the drag tension on Jenny's little reel--it was functioning perfectly--and told her not to crank it unless the fish ran toward her. "Just keep a bend in your rod to pressure the fish. The odds are in his favor, and this is going to take a while, maybe over an hour," I warned her.

After a quarter of an hour Jenny was noticeably fatigued, but the fish still held upstream fighting both his small, determined adversary and the hard current. Then the fish turned downstream, a rooster-tail of water sizzling from the line following in his wake. Fully visible to us, the giant fish made two revolutions around the pool. Then, with diamond-shaped spots on its glowing back lit by bright afternoon sun, the Chinook was swimming hard against strong current before it stationed in the glassy tail of the pool, at the lip above the foamy rapids, and was still clearly visible more than halfway across the river.

Jenny shrieked, "Oh my God, it's going to go down the rapids!" She had judged the fish's intention correctly and her own dwindling chances of successfully landing it. I gritted my teeth and tried to look calm as the fish backed over the lip and into white water. Instantly Jenny's line hung up on a dishwasher-size boulder in the middle of the river. I reached down and backed off the drag knob on her reel releasing tension to keep the line from breaking. Then, in fast water up to my crotch I was barely able to lift the line over the rock only to find it hung around another larger boulder in the swiftest part of the rapids downstream from the clump of broken alders.

Jenny probably weighed about 100 pounds. It was all I could do to pick her up and wade the river carrying her in my arms. The current ran at a fair speed over the uneven bottom. Somehow, we made it through. I stood her on the bank downstream of the alders. The foaming rapids were waist deep. Jenny handed me her wading staff and I inched my way into the river over a bottom of big rocks, many dangerously loose enough to roll underfoot. The current was pushing against the small of my back and I could only stay put with help from the wading staff. I still couldn't reach high enough to free the line from the boulder. Carefully shifting position to keep my balance I used the staff to extend my reach. The line came free. The salmon was still hooked, but far downstream, holding in the lower pool. It took several minutes for me to get back to shore, and even longer to carry Jenny downstream into a position even with the fish. When we finally got there, I spotted a giant boulder that rose from the edge of the river. At some time in its ancient history a piece had broken off, and years of rolling to its present position had shaped it into a perfect waterfront chair. I lifted Jenny into it.

The big salmon had been hooked for over half an hour and the thin line had abraded in several places when the fish came through the rapids. I figured his teeth had also cut into the line, and how that tiny hook had held this long was beyond me. Jenny was running out of gas and complaining she was hurting from the exertion. The longer the fight lasted, the less chance we had of landing that fish. I coached Jenny as best I could and offered support and encouragement, "Just a little longer. See he's tiring. You've almost got him. Great job. Hang on. We'll get him landed."

Still, the battle lasted for another half an hour, the fish seesawing back and forth, and up and down the pool. Finally, the fish was tired and docile enough to grab him by the wrist of his broad tail. Placing my other hand under his wide belly, I lifted him from the water and set him across Jenny's lap. She handed me her camera, and I snapped several quick pictures before placing the fish back in the water. The tiny treble hook I thought too small to hold such a fish was lodged between the tongue and gum and wrapped so tightly in skin I had to cut it out with my knife. After what seemed a long time, the Chinook gained back its strength, and I released it back into the river to carry out its mission. As the image of that huge spotted fish melted into the depths of the clear, clean pool, and the improbability of the day's events cascaded through my mind, I was reminded that the age of magic still exists where wild things live in wild places. Jenny was as tired as the fish and had to be carried back to the van. She smiled faintly and said, "Great job. We did it. We have lived my dream. Thank you. Thank you."

A week later, a manila envelope arrived in the mail. Inside was an 8 X10 glossy of a dark-haired lady under a wide brimmed hat shading a grin nearly as wide, the grand live salmon resting across her bare thighs. In one corner, in delicate penmanship, she had written, Love, Jenny.

Chapter 17

Sport Fishing Tribalism

We exist in a bizarre combination of Stone Age emotions, medieval beliefs, and god-like technology.

-- E.O. Wilson

Anglers love to divide into factions to make themselves look wise, and other fishers look stupid. It often back-fires. It's: nymph vs. swing, wet vs. dry, Spey vs. single, barbed vs. barbless, hatchery vs. wild, etc. There seems to be plenty in the sport of angling to argue about. The commercial fish killers must enjoy our disharmony, it's kind of like the Irish Clans battling each other in front of the Vikings,

Fly Fishers vs. Gear Heads

It was September, primetime, 2001, the year when over 600,000 summer Steelhead migrated upstream through the Bonneville Dam's fish ladders. As opposed to the early 2020's, the Deschutes River was loaded with Steelhead!

In the drift boat days, in the decades before this

story, I could always tell which camps were catching Steelhead by listening as we floated by. Like birds in the thickets, anglers are boisterous when they are having fun and quiet when they are not. Our camp had been full of laughter during the late morning brunch, then suddenly it went deathly quiet. I heard the stroke of an oar and the splash of boots hitting the water. I took a couple of steps, looked over the steep bank, and saw a yellow raft pull-in behind our two parked jet boats. A pair of spin gear fishers were in our camp water. Neither acknowledged our presence.

A growly voice from inside our screen house said, "Look at that, those bastards are fishing our camp water." Admittedly those intruders were annoying. And they had undoubtedly broken an unwritten rule of good etiquette, "*Never fish anyone's camp water without first asking permission.*" Also, in my mind they had done so with malice of forethought knowing it would cause friction. By any civilized code, their actions were provocative and rude.

Where there had been celebration and comradery all morning, there was now a steady stream of grumbling from our eight clients. I stuck my head in the tent and was met by a challenge, "Bachmann, what are you going to do about those two ass holes in our camp water?" The question came from a client who had been drooling over my vintage, long barrel, Colt Python revolver the evening before. My reply came easily in a low voice, "I'm going to my tent, get my 357, and I'm going to leave a couple of corpses lying in the water full of maggots as a warning to the next intruders." I ducked back out of the tent. Instantly, someone from inside hollered, "Wait…wait, you can't do that!" Then I fully entered the tent and stood at the head of the table. "Of course, I am not going to do that, but it is tempting. This is public water. They literally have as much right to fish this water as we do. Maybe you would like it better if I stood on the bank and bitched at them." Then I asked, "how many fish did you catch this morning?" The answers were mixed, but everyone had landed at least one Steelhead. Most had hooked several and one guy had landed three. The problem wasn't competition for fish. My crew had all met their goals that morning. The sun was full on the water and no one from our group had fished in the last two hours. I added to our conversation, "In less than forty five minutes those guys will be gone and you will never see them again." Actually, the gear heads hung around for only twenty minutes, caught no fish, got ignored, got apprehensive, lost interest, and left. The warm, friendly conversation resumed when the raft departed. The incident was not discussed further in camp.

The crazy thing is that if the two invaders had been using Spey tackle or had asked permission to trespass into our camp when they landed, all eight clients would have helped them tie up their boat and let them know where each fish had been caught and what flies had been productive that same morning. But since they were obviously from a different tribe and were ill-mannered, they were instantly labeled as enemies.

A client of mine named Bob tried to persuade me that many gear fishermen on the Sandy River, fishing during the winter, wouldn't low-hole a fly fisher if the fly fishing methodology were explained to them in a nice way. And he was right some of the time. They didn't understand that we intended to start at the top of a run and fish our way through it. Once the methodology was explained, they would be fine at going to the back of the line. Most were cooperative, but some were not. Some wanted to test whether their method was in fact superior and see if they could catch Steelhead from water a Spey angler had already fished. But some also recounted getting into the water two hundred yards downstream of a fly fisher and getting yelled at. Fly fishers aren't always warm and fuzzy either. Quiet, non-threatening conversation is often a good first step in solving territorial disputes.

Fishing Guides vs. The General Public

Macho, territorial, greedy fishing guides can exhibit poor examples for the angling public to follow. Fly fishing is a competitive sport if you are a guide. Getting your clients set up in a productive, easy to fish, section of well rested water, to start every day, is the goal of most Steelhead guides. On desert rivers such as the Deschutes, many trips start an hour before light with each guide navigating the river by sound. Once arriving at the morning water, territory is held with a flashlight or headlamp to let other anglers know that the spot is taken. One well known, female, fly fishing guide started hanging head lamps in her favorite morning water the evening before. The price of her morning water was a set of new AAA batteries each day. Several anglers caught on to her routine, and using lightweight single person boats, would launch straight across the river and use her light to navigate by, and beat her to the spot. They then stole her head lamps. There is a whole tribe of anglers who have a dislike for professional guides and purposely screw with them every chance, as a hobby. There are also certain guides who deserve anglers' disdain by thinking they are aristocracy and should have special privileges on public water.

Halford vs. Skues

Frederick Maurice Halford and George Edward Mackenzie Skues fished for trout on the chalk streams of southern England in the mid-1800's to the early 1900's. Their favorite was The Itchen, the same stream favored by Izaak Walton and Dame Julianna Berners hundreds of years earlier. This geographic area can rightly be called the birthplace of fly fishing for trout as a science and sport. Halford was a proponent of the upstream cast, natural floating, dry fly methods and helped develop hooks, leaders, and tapered fly lines to facilitate that style of fishing. He turned it from a method to a dogma. Halford was an able writer and he and his readers turned dry fly fishing for trout from a dogma into a religion for many anglers worldwide.

Skues, on the other hand, fished the complete hatch: nymph, emerger, dun, cripple, and sunk spinner on the same water. Whether Skues was a better person or technician than Halford is unknown, but it is clear that he was a better scientist. However, Halford was a better politician. He was able to make many anglers believe that fishing close to the surface is closer to God than fishing deep. It is hard to argue how God would see it. But if limiting your impact on the fishery and leveling the playing field in favor of the trout is the goal of fly fishing, then he would probably give the nod. You will hook fewer fish if you are a dry fly purest.

Bill McMillan vs. Jim Teeny

I got the call at about 10 in the morning on a Saturday. The easy to understand, positive, exuberant, perfect diction and boyish enthusiasm was easy to identify. It was Jim Teeny calling to set up a walking trip on the Salmon River mid-August 1988. He wanted a trip for three, but one was a non-fishing photographer. Two would be fishing, he would be one of them and he wouldn't need help. The other angler would be Michael Fong, a writer from San Francisco. The photographer would be Mike's wife Christine. Could I get Mike into some Steelhead so Christine could photograph him? I said, "Yes, I can make it happen! There are lots of Steelhead in the river, but the water is very low and clear. The fish are timid.

"Can we be on the water by 5:00 A.M.?" I asked.

His reply was, "I never get up at 5:00 for anything."

I tried to convince him, "We've been getting fish but most of them at first light."

Jim wasn't having any of it," Let's meet at the Barlow Trail Inn for breakfast at 9:00am
." End of conversation. We were meeting for breakfast.

A year earlier, Bill McMillan had published *Dry Line Steelhead and Other Subjects*. It recounted Bill's adventures of catching Steelhead year-round with a single hand fly rod and floating fly line. Bill has a smooth, easy style of writing and fishing, backed by a lot of tradition. His methodology caught on with many anglers belonging to the "aristocratic" set. And with good reason. His whole stance was very genteel. I bought into it and was using similar methods to catch summer Steelhead, which was what was on my mind when Jim Teeny hired me on the phone. I was unaware at the time that there was intense controversy between the floating line McMillan crowd and the sunk line teeny advocates. Though we had met, I didn't know much about Jim Teeny at the time.

I couldn't conceive that fly fishing in the middle of the day, in the bright sunshine, was realistic or productive for most cold-water fish. I arrived at the Barlow Trail Inn at 8:45. Jim arrived at 9:30 and ordered breakfast. On the exterior I tried to be pleasant and serine. On the Inside my head is spinning with WTF!? I kept it all bottled up, but it just seemed that the situation was becoming worse by the minute. Jim was in no hurry. By the time we left the restaurant it was after 11:00. I led the party to a piece of private land. There we parked a hundred yards from the river. Jim showed the landowner every new piece of fly-fishing equipment he had with him. By the time we got to the river it was noon and there were three bait fishermen in the pool. Jim walked up to them in a friendly fashion and asked how they were doing. They admitted to having been there since daylight and had no bites. I surveyed the pool from the top of a huge boulder at the head end. There were a dozen bright Steelhead suspended in the flow near the bottom. The bait fishers left, walking downstream, and I motioned Jim up to me. He immediately saw the fish and asked if he could try. He hooked and landed a twelve pounder on his second cast. It was the first of three fish he landed from that pool. Mike, Christine, and I crossed the river, and I spotted a Steelhead parked in the shade under an overhanging tree branch. After a couple of small jumps, it came off. It was Mike's only fish of the day. Meanwhile, Jim went 9 for 12. Both men had comparable casting skills and the flies were similar. I think the difference was Jim’s fly line sank so much quicker and that he had nearly superhuman eyesight. He was able to track his fly and fish it dead drift into the strike zone of the fish, which was very small.

This chapter is not written to prove the validity of one method over the other or to take sides in the conflicts which arose between the two methods or the two anglers. In the chapter above, Jim got to pick the time and the terrain, and he wisely did so to his advantage. To me, fly fishing is a scientific experiment that teaches the angler about fish. There are many discussions about whether the fly pattern is most important. Jim's method, as displayed above, tends to substantiate what I call the "*convenience factor*", which states: The fly closest to a fish's mouth is the one that gets eaten.

If we had gone fishing during the low light hours, Mike would have caught more fish and Jim may have caught less. I am betting Jim would have still caught the most because I have fished with Jim during many trips when he had to read the water and fish blind on water where fish weren't visible to anyone, and he was able to hold his own. The only time I personally out-fished Jim was when I used a Spey rod, and he used a single hander. We were fishing for winter Steelhead on large water and my ability to cover more water made the difference.

And the supposed conflict between Jim and Bill and their fishing methods that was such a leading topic of the 1990's? It was mostly a contrivance of other anglers who probably didn't know either man or either method very well. Such is often the case in many disputes.

Chapter 18
How Much is a Fishing Guide Worth?

"A goal is not always meant to be reached.
It often serves simply as something to aim at."
– Bruce Lee

The names of the people are fictitious; the personalities, circumstances, situations, years, and geography are real.

In my Steelhead fly fishing camp on Oregon's Deschutes River are three generations of a powerful family of Scottish descent, the MacLeods. The MacLeods are mannerly, pragmatic, hard-working, and undisputedly honest to the letter of the law. They are also well-connected and successful businesspeople. All three generations were born and raised in Central Oregon. The patriarch Abel, born in 1910, grew up on the family homestead. He worked his way through college and became a CPA. He survived the Great Depression, inherited the family farm, and turned it into a 25,000-acre cattle ranch.

Bran, Abel's son, and my contact with the MacLeod clan was born in 1937. After graduating from college with an MBA, he was recruited by the food processing giant, R.J. Simplot, the company who made Idaho potato products internationally available. After a couple of years at Simplot, he decided to go into business for himself. Bran hit it big in commodities and currently employs 200 people. While still in college, he married his high school sweetheart Nancy. Nancy was a Rose Festival Queen thirty plus years ago and is now an Oregon State Senator representing the downtown district of Portland, Oregon. Bran and Nancy had two children, Conon their firstborn and then their daughter, Nelly . Like his father and grandfather, Conon graduated from college with degrees in business and accounting. It became clear that Conon was a financial prodigy. He went to college for eight years and made a minimum of $250,000 per year from his own investments while in school. Upon graduation, Conon was recruited by Merrill Lynch at $450,000 per year plus benefits to manage Ted Turner's finances. Eventually, Conon was sent to China to run Merrill Lynch's Hong Kong operation. China's economy took off. He made himself and his partners filthy rich. When Conon returned to the US seven years later, Merrill Lynch handed him the reins to their new High-Tech Division. With his success, Conon bought the Rockefeller Mansion for 7.5 million in cash and then sunk another 10 million into it in renovations.

Fast forward to Conon and his friends' guided fly-fishing trips. I charged each of these gentlemen $350 per day to take them fishing in an aluminum drift boat, large and seaworthy enough to float them and all the camp gear down the river comfortably and safely for four days at a time.

I tore down our camp every morning and set it up again, downriver, each afternoon. I did the cooking, maintenance, and domestic chores, and served as the communication network, intel, and logistics. I was the pack leader, keeping the pack moving and hunting.

I did not employ an extra person with a second boat to deal with the camp and cooking because it would have added complexity to logistics and might have slowed us down. I strategized to cover water by the cubic mile. At this time, there were few competitors for camp sites or fishing water. Trips were barely less intense than full blown military search and destroy missions. Success was less about social networking and more about numbers of fish landed and released. Every team member was expected to be in good physical condition and be able to fish from dawn to dark, and each member was expected to contribute to the total numbers of the team. We traversed both sides of a big river at the rate of about five miles a day and fished nearly everything that was fishable with a fly.

Lunches were eaten on the run. We racked up what would seem in the future impossible scores. The MacLeods were hard physical men with intense can-do attitudes.

The days were long, and the work was very physical. I supplied the food and camping gear included in the trip's price. I grossed $1,050 per day, $4,200 per trip, and $25,000 a month in 1988. I was young and ambitious. My position would look like a pretty good deal if that were the whole story. However, unfortunately, it was not.

Because of changing weather and water conditions, fluctuating fish runs, and client unreliability, my calendar is often half full. Also, there are plenty of entities who view this kind of income as if it were a milk run. Suddenly instead of a fellow human being, they see me as a cow to be milked. Federal, State, and county governments think they deserve to be fed. They dictate how much, and that alone can be 35%. Then there is insurance, loan interest, fuel for the tow vehicle, and a shuttle driver. Add to those mechanic bills, and propane for stoves and lanterns. Rather quickly, I'm down another 15%. Before you know it, take-home pay has dwindled to 50% of gross. If a tow vehicle or boat trailer succumbs to the wash-board access road, or tents get shattered by extra-strong winds, wages further go down in a hurry. Instead of grossing $25,000 per month, I am down to half of that. However, I believe I am still in a pretty good position.

The MacLeods are congenial, well-organized, and capable fly fishers. Annoyingly though, they are poor tippers. Many of my groups give me an extra $100 per day, $400 for the trip. Tips fuel my winter vacation fund. But the MacLeods only give me an additional $100 for the entire trip or sometimes forget to tip altogether. After five years of busting my buns to win them over, I have lost interest. Whether they know it or not, I am no longer giving them my best. Even though they take ten days a year off my calendar at the standard rate, I know there are better-paying clients. Subconsciously, I am looking for a way to break the news without alienating them.

Tonight, we are gathered in my dining room screen house after dinner, sitting around the folding dining table and sipping on their fifth of 25-year-old Glenlivet Special Reserve ($2,000 per bottle). After my second wee dram, just enough to lubricate my vocal cords, I asked, "I know you guys have all fished this river before you knew me. How come you spend all this money on my wages? You could buy the equipment and do it yourself and save a bunch of money?"

I can see by the look on Abel's face; my

question has annoyed him. At 78 and having a reputation as an impatient man, his conversation is often short, to the point, bordering on rude—especially when talking to anyone he thinks to be needlessly stupid.

"You have no idea how it works," is his reply. "In the price of the equipment, you don't cost us anything. We get you for free."

The harmony and cheer of the mood are instantly gone. The atmosphere turns dead quiet. Suddenly I am stone sober and reply quietly, "I find that hard to believe?"

My eyes meet Bran's across the table. "It is true," he says. "We did a lengthy study on that exact question. We concluded that if we bought all the equipment in partnership it takes to do these trips ourselves, it would take 17 ½ days to break even with hiring a guide. We knew we only had ten days a year to go Steelhead fishing. After that, our only decision was 'Which guide do we hire?'"

I was in disbelief. After all, how many times does anyone offer to explain how your hard work has no value? Though that wasn't blatantly said, it meant the same to me. I purposely kept my voice unemotional and asked if anyone would like to show me how that might be true. Abel said he would be glad too, and he instructed me to get a tablet and something to write with. When I had done so, he advised me to form three columns and label them: Subject, Cost, and Length of Depreciation. In the first vertical column, he told me to write: Tow Vehicle, Boat & Trailer, Storage for Boat, Trailer & Vehicle, Fuel, Shuttles, Tents, Cots & Pads, Kitchen, Tables, Lanterns, Shuttles, Propane, Batteries, Food, Water, and Coolers. Then he said, "I have a lot of room to store equipment but am planning to sell the ranch, so soon I won't. These two guys (he gestured) live in town, and Conon lives clear across the country. None of us have a place to store a trailered boat or camp gear."

It didn't take long for me to figure out that these ole' boys might not know a lot about navigating rivers with a drift boat or finding Steelhead, but they got wealthy by paying attention to some things that I didn't do very well.

Abel laid out a game plan, "Unless you are in business, never spend money on anything that depreciates or is not deductible. That includes cars, trucks, boats, airplanes, and women—unless they are wives. If it flies, floats, or fucks, rent it!"

If you are in business or plan to be in business, and guiding is a business, you better know something about the rules of business. After being in the fly-fishing guide business for over forty years, it looks a lot different to me now than when I started. And after employing other guides, the game is not what it appears to be at all. Most beginners think that the primary skill is being able to catch fish. That is an essential but peripheral skill.

If you were to approach me for advice about becoming a fishing guide, the first thing I would tell you is to go to college and get a business degree. That advice would also be the same if you wanted to be a self-employed mechanic, farmer, artist, or any other profession. First, get a business degree. Because no matter what you want to do for income, you are your own business. You cannot be successful at being self-employed without having an education. The United States of America, which is explained as "the land of the free and the brave," died before WWII. In the modern era, a tremendous amount of the population works for federal, state, or county governments or receives financial assistance from the same. Government permits, licenses, regulations, and taxes pervade everything. It is on the shoulders of businesses (especially small businesses) to pay for everything. This includes employee withholding, Federal Income Tax, State Income Tax, SAIF, Social Security, etc. There are usually a host of other fees such as boat ramp fees, parking fees, fishing licenses, harvest tags, and the list goes on and on. However, most of these licenses and fees are tax-deductible. Vehicles, trailers, and boats depreciate, and the depreciation is deductible. Don't forget insurance. Your guide license and permits to use any kind of state or federal land will require proof of liability insurance with the license vendor and/or permit holder named on your insurance. Although from a "free thinker's" point of view, you may think hiring a person to run a second boat would be your first employee. It is not. The first person that your guide corporation hires is yourself. The second is a bookkeeper. Your third is a tax accountant. If you are smart, you will hire an attorney to set the business up as an S-Corp or LLC, so you are legal and in compliance with all government entities. Being able to run a guide business not only involves handling money but also navigating the logistics of equipment, food, and everything that dictates your client's comfort and safety. For you or your clients, a perfect day of fishing does not end stopped along a lonely road at midnight with a burnt-out boat trailer wheel bearing. You better learn how to keep all your equipment clean and in perfect working order.

After learning to run a business, teaching fly casting, identifying, and catching fish isn't the second most important skill set to master. It is being socially astute. Learn how to market your business and network and communicate with your established clients. There are no better clients than the ones that you already have. Many of the people you take fishing will appear to be wealthy and secure, and as a result, they may never admit that social connection is the essence of their game. Your clients will all run in packs. Their power is in introducing other members of their tribe to something good. If they bring their buddies to your camp and you do something that embarrasses them in front of their sphere of influence, like smelling like marijuana or saying the word fuck, they will never hire you again, and they will never tell you why.

The discussion about the business of guiding was all learned the hard way as I am naturally proud, curious, and edgy. Because of that, I watched less capable guides gloat over stealing my clientele. In some cases, I was too edgy to be around. But in many cases, they were clients that didn't suit me anyhow. From a pure business standpoint, if you want to make maximum money, accept all paying customers, and disregard all their crap. Most people try to be good company and are fair in all they do. Work hard to keep those clients as they will be the majority. However, some prospective clients are incapable of considering your needs. My basic rule is that a client can be disagreeable or a poor tipper, but they can't be both. The next time they try to hire me, I'm booked solid for years. Then I hand them business cards from my least likable competitors.

Every state regulates its guides differently. In states like Montana, guides that agreed on a monopoly on a river years ago became Outfitters. They are allowed to promote their businesses and have accrued much value in these state agreements. Such agreements can be worth hundreds of thousands or

work on most Montana rivers is to be employed by an Outfitter who has a permit on that river. That Outfitter may employ many guides and are responsible for all their taxes, insurance, equipment, state law compliance, regulations, and guide training. There is a certain freedom from drudgery and responsibility in that arrangement for the guides. In states such as Oregon, every guide is licensed individually. Guide businesses don't accrue value the same as in Montana. In Oregon, no Outfitter has a monopoly on any geographic area. Instead, revenues are distributed to guides directly.

While in Bozeman, Montana, one fall, I asked a fly shop owner about the wages he paid to his guides. The answer was fifty bucks a day. When asked how he could get by with that, he answered that applicants were usually so naïve as not to know the difference, so why not exploit them? I couldn't believe that any guide in Oregon would be that naïve, having to pay for liability insurance, a guide license, and a Red Cross First Aid/CPR class. Nor could I believe that clients would want to hire an ill-advised guide to take them fishing. From my standpoint, even having a business plan based on that kind of inequity is unrealistic. It demands that everyone involved, except for the Outfitter, is dull, including the clientele. Who would want to form a long-term relationship with a guide or outfitter group where relationships were excessively lopsided? Though, apparently, it worked for them. The guy had a big, prosperous-looking, well-stocked fly shop with lots of satisfied-looking customer traffic. To my knowledge, twenty years later, he is still in business. Perhaps many fishing guides and the anglers who hire them aren't like selective trout.

The great entertainer P.T. Barnum might have been right when he said, "There's a sucker born every minute." We're all hoping we weren't one of them.

Chapter 19

Lessons in Catch and Release

"Life is never fair,

and perhaps it is a good thing for most of us that it is not."

--Oscar Wilde

The formative years were the 1950's on a cattle ranch encompassing a mile long stretch of prime trout stream in the Idaho Panhandle. We owned the finest stretch of Grouse Creek, the best spawning/rearing tributary in the Lake Pend Oreille basin during its heyday when it regularly produced giant Kamloops and Bull Trout, some over thirty pounds. Trout and char migrated from the huge natural lake into tributaries for reproduction during spring and fall much like salmon and steelhead in rivers which have access to the Ocean. The major staging pool was thirty feet behind our second barn, which was nearly in the center of the property. There were only four anglers allowed to fish our water. I was one of them. We each fished a couple days a week. The other three anglers never took home more than three fish each, just enough for one meal. Without me knowing, they were setting a standard.

As a tradition, my trout were caught, killed, dressed, and laid to rest in my fern lined wicker creel and brought home for my family to consume. In the beginning, the heavier the creel the more praise I received. Most of the trout I caught were 2 to 4 pounds.

As time went on and my skills improved, a daily catch was often more than we needed, and trout started stacking up in our freezer to become a burden. They weren't near as tasty after being frozen for a couple of weeks as they were when fresh caught. My parents grew up in the great depression. Nothing was ever wasted.

To me fishing was more than just an acquisition of protein, it was recreation and a way to study nature. There was a steady reliable supply of fish. It was easy for me to turn some loose.

I was introduced to the concept of "Catch and Release" as a fishing ethic and management tool while watching a TV program called "American Sportsman." The episode that got my attention featured Lee Wulff fishing for Atlantic Salmon in Labrador, Canada. After landing a large salmon on a tiny fly rod, he let it go explaining, "A wild gamefish is too valuable to be caught only once". Lee Wulff became one of my boyhood heroes. Starting in the

1970's catch and release was heavily promoted by Trout Unlimited. By then I had moved to Oregon and became a steelhead angler. At first steelhead were hard for me to catch and were a treat for my wife and young kids and they all celebrated when a steelhead was brought home. Then through the glory days of the 1980's steelhead began to stack up in our freezer. Catch and release started to make even more sense to me then, but not to everyone. That ethic is more easily understood by anglers who regularly catch more fish than they want to eat.

One day while fishing the Pipeline Hole on the Sandy River with about ten other fishermen I landed a buck steelhead and released it. A guy fishing next to me asked, "Wha'd you do that for."

My reply, "I didn't need it."

His reply, "Bull shit, I'm keep'n mine."

My reply with a grin, "First, you gotta' catch one."

The primordial hunter/gatherer instinct runs deep in humans. In the age of "Artificial Intelligence," corporate agriculture, and super stores with nearly endless supplies of packaged things to eat, many humans want to believe they can still survive and prosper in a natural world by living off the land. I doubt if it is so; humans have been far too successful at reproducing. Naturally occurring harvest fisheries are nearly a thing of the past in most parts of the world. "Catch and Release" makes more sense now than when I was a kid growing up and only having to share fishing water with three other anglers who understood how fragile wild fisheries are.

But not everyone agrees with "Catch and Release" and sometimes it can get downright contentious. The Sandy River winter steelhead run of 1979/80 was the largest ever recorded and was estimated at 16,000 fish. In February 1980 Murlin Gregg and I were still building a few houses even though there was a bad economic recession. Work was intermittent and one week in February 1980 we fished every day. Then as today certain sections of the Sandy are regulated that boats can be used for transportation, but fishing from a floating device is not allowed. Murlin and I each owned 17' Alumiweld drift boats and each day we swapped boats. Monday, he rowed, Tuesday I rowed, etc. Then it was Friday and his turn to row again. Fishing was always a friendly, supportive, but competitive, numbers game between us. In those days we both fished with all kinds of tackle. That week he used a 5001C ambassador level wind reel on a graphite casting rod, and I used a 9' 9-weight fiberglass fly rod with a sinking shooting head fly line. He had out-fished me every day that week, but Friday was my day. And it turned out to be the best day of fly fishing for winter steelhead I've ever had. I had landed nine steelhead by the time we got to the gravel-bar island at the mouth of Big Creek, halfway through our float. There I landed another steelhead and hooked a huge winter Chinook. It was much too large for my steelhead tackle and would have spooled me, except Murlin rowed me to the other side of the river where I could follow the fish on foot. The boat was landed upstream from a right-angle river bend where four anglers were fishing. They graciously reeled in and allowed us to pass. At that point, the Chinook was still far downstream under a full head of steam. Two of the four anglers stashed their gear and followed us to enjoy the show. One angler was small, and I don't remember much about him. The other was a Nordic type about six foot four, white haired, rangy, athletic looking, in a red wool plaid mackinaw jacket and hip boots. He had the agility and confident bearing of a retired logger...probably a choker setter or a tree faller, or maybe even a logging company owner. Everyone was pleasant, enjoying the angler and the big fish. Finally, after nearly an hour we reached a wide sandbar where the kids at Camp Collins played volleyball during the summer. The Chinook was huge, maybe thirty-five pounds. It was sexually immature with a broad back colored dark purplish green and sides like polished silver. Finally, it was exhausted, and I waded ten feet from the bank into crotch deep water and was able to tail the fish against my hip, remove the hook from its mouth, let it regain its strength, and release it.

It was then that a loud shrill male voice behind me said, "What the fuck! You let it go! Why'd you let it go?" I turned around to face the shore. It was the big guy in the red jacket, who was now obviously very unhappy.

My adrenaline was rising, but I stayed calm and replied in as friendly a manner as I could muster, "That was a very rare fish. I didn't want to kill that fish. We're better off with that fish in the river, besides, you can catch your own fish."

His reply, "I've been fishing this river for years and never caught a steelhead. If you didn't want that fish, you could have given it to me." His voice rose in octaves and pitch and his face was turning red, "I've never seen a fish like that!" His voice rose to an even higher pitch.

I replied, "Like I said that was a very rare Winter Chinook…and old timers told me there used to be many more of them. Besides, I couldn't keep that fish, I'm already limited out."

His reply, "What do you mean you're limited out? How many fish have you caught today?"

It often amazes me after an escapade like this,

how inept I can be and how difficult it is for me to keep my mouth shut. I had just had the best day of fishing in my life and was pumped up about it. My reply was, “I’ve landed ten steelhead today plus that Chinook.”

The red jacket guy exploded with frustration, “Ten Steelhead, ten steelhead, I ought’ a kick your ass!”

My adrenaline shot to full charge. I was extremely vulnerable, knee deep in the river, with a much larger, probably stronger, insane sounding opponent, who was at a higher elevation on the riverbank. My instincts told me to ditch the rod and get out of the water. I grabbed the rod like a javelin to throw it into the bushes on the bank. My only exit was where “Red Jacket” was standing. Moving as fast as possible in knee deep water and throwing the rod reel-first as hard as I could, I came boiling out of the river. The throw was good, but the first stripping guide nicked my index finger, which altered the trajectory and Red Jacket ducked or my heavy steelhead reel would have struck him in the forehead. I was still coming when Red Jacket lost his nerve turned on his heel and started walking at a fast pace upriver toward his stashed rod. I realized the confrontation was over and regained my composure. Murlin’s boat was still upstream, so we had to follow Red

Jacket and his little buddy.

About every hundred yards he would lament, "God damn, can you believe that guy turned that fuckin' fish loose?"

A few years later my wife Patty and I started a fly-fishing business, and most fly fishers are into conservation and "Catch and Release". People tend to gravitate to other likeminded folks. After a while it is easy to believe that all the population agrees with you. Then occasionally, something happens that jerks you back to reality.

The old man and the little redheaded girl might have been the most unlikely pair of anglers that ever sat in my old aluminum drift boat. He was a past seventy, white haired, composed, soft, out of shape big city lawyer. She was fourteen, naturally curly red haired, pimpled, freckled, short, squatty, but full of enthusiasm and energy. She wore a big sterling, six-pointed star hung from a leather thong around her neck and was the product of the old man's second marriage, which had come late in life. Although physical beauty had passed her by, there was the light of strength and resolve that shown through her bright blue eyes. Both clients said they had never fly fished before but expected that with my help catching a couple of winter steelhead shouldn't be too difficult.

I dropped the boat off the trailer, loaded the gear, parked my rig, got my clients settled-in, and rowed them across the river to a large island upstream of the boat ramp.

Flanking this Island was the best fly fishing riffl e in the whole river. Oregon Department of Fish and Wildlife planted big numbers of young hatchery steelhead at the ramp in those days and after spending a couple of years in the Pacific Ocean many returned to the riffle, which was a couple of hundred yards upstream of the ramp. If it was unoccupied, I started every morning there. A predictable scene unfolded as I did my best to teach my two new clients how to use the two Spey rods, I had loaned to them. The old man was worn out in the first ten minutes. A life of carpeted offices and city sidewalks had left him unprepared for any exertion in the out of doors. The girl although not a quick learner, started to grasp the principles of fly casting. At least she was trying. After an hour both clients were ready for a boat ride and a change of scenery.

We left the island and as the boat floated downstream, I noticed a man playing a steelhead near the boat ramp. He was a tall, slim fellow in hip boots and was using a spinning rod. I rowed gently against the current and held the boat in place, figuring that it might be the only steelhead my clients might see that day. When the angler finally got the fish into shallow water, he kicked it out onto the beach where it flopped around and was soon covered with sand. Just as suddenly he reached down and broke his leader and kicked the fish back into the water.

In our rivers all wild steelhead are protected and must be released unharmed. Hatchery fish may be harvested. As a staunch advocate of such laws, I enquired of the guy if that fish had been a wild one. He replied that it had been and that he was sick and tired of catching wild steelhead and he wanted a “keeper”. I replied that the fish he had treated so inhumanely was a living animal and should be accorded more respect. His reply was that it was just a fish and didn’t matter. That’s when I lost my cool and asked him how he would like it if someone rolled him around on a sand bar and kicked his ass in the water. He flipped me off.

About twenty or thirty quick hard pulls on the oars brought my boat quickly to his area of the beach hard enough that it hit the sand with a thud. In the same motion I was out of the boat and running at the guy who turned and fled, running up the paved road to the parking lot with me in hot pursuit. I was halfway up the hill when I realized that I hadn’t taken the time to drop the anchor and the boat with my passengers might be floating down the river without me at the oars. I stopped, looked around and sure enough it was. I had to let the guy go.

When I got back to the boat it had only moved a little way downstream and getting in was easy. My blood pressure was still up but subsiding. The old man was trembling with fear in his eyes. However, it was evident that his daughter had enjoyed the whole scene.

"Too bad I didn't know how to work the anchor," she said with a big grin, "It would have been interesting to see what would have happened if you'da caught him!"

We crossed the river again and floated down a backchannel behind another big island. This channel was nearly a quarter mile long with the first and last hundred yards being the best steelhead water. The last hundred were often the best of the best.

We fished the first hundred yards with no luck, but it seemed as though the redhead was learning how to cast. Then we floated to the second stretch. I placed the Old Man at the top of the run where wading was easier. Then took the girl to the lower middle of the run. A large flat submerged boulder made a vee shaped slick in the otherwise choppy riffle. Previous clients had landed several steelhead from that slick during preceding trips that season. A

Bead Head Black Bunny Leech was attached to the end of the short, stout leader. The barb on the hook had been mashed down.

We walked upstream of the boulder where we discussed a game plan that would swing the fly in concentric arcs through the slick. On the third cast her rod bent down under the pressure of a very hard strike and a bright silver fish with a nearly black back rocketed through the surface of the water multiple times pulling line off the reel while racing up stream where it nearly ran into the girl's father while splashing water all over him. Then the fish came back down stream against a totally slack line. I offered instructions, but to no avail as there was too much going on for the girl to cope with. Finally, she was able to retrieve all of the line and to our relief the fish was still connected to it. When the fish was finally in my net, examination disclosed the barbless fly and leader had gone clear through the maxillary muscle from the inside and the hook was stuck in the fish's gill plate on the outside. The leader was threaded through the corner of the fish's jaw. No way that fish could have come free unless the leader had broken. The eight pound steelhead was missing its adipose fin which marked it of hatchery origin and legal to harvest. The fish was kept submerged in the net until it was examined by both my clients. Then upon agreement, it was dispatched, butchered, and put into a clean plastic bag so they could take it home. The rest of the day on the water was comparatively uneventful.

The phone rang as soon as I walked through the front door at home. It was Bill Doran, park manager where we had launched the boat that morning. In those days upper echelon park employees were deputized to enforce fish and game laws. Bill and I had always got along very well, but in this conversation his voice had an icy edge to it as he explained that he had driven to the boat launch parking lot about ten o'clock that morning. Upon arriving, an out of breath man ran up to his pickup while jabbering that some crazy man had jumped out of his drift boat and had chased him up the hill. "When I asked him to describe the boat and the person it sounded a lot like you. Was it you Mark? You can't be assaulting our guests, Mark!"

I admitted that it was me. Then asked, "Would you like to hear my side of the story,
Bill?"

He said that he would listen to what I had to say, and I explained what had happened.

"He solemnly said the stories matched. Then his voice brightened and said, "That's when I showed him my badge and told him that if I ever caught him treating fish that way, I would arrest him!" Then he laughed. His mean guy act had all been for show, and I could tell he had really enjoyed putting pressure on me. We ended the conversation as friends and had a good laugh.

Forward to a couple of weeks later. I was with another pair of anglers but doing the same routine, rowing across the river, then up to the island. These guys were experienced and one hooked and landed a steelhead on his first cast of the morning, a very, very rare event. After half an hour we were ready to go down river. Déjà vu. The angler I had chased was at the boat ramp with another steelhead hooked up. He had his back to us. I don't believe he knew we were there, and I was getting mentally prepared for what I expected was going to be another confrontational episode. His fish was led into shallow water and tailed with a glove. The hook was removed with a pair of pliers. The fish was released without ever touching the bank. It swam away easily. Then the angler stood up and turned around obviously surprised to see us. His expression changed to uncertainty as he recognized me. I extended my hand an held up my thumb while looking him straight in the eyes with a genuine smile. He returned the gesture. All is well that ends well.

Chapter 20

The Lunch Spot

Two things are infinite: the universe and human stupidity. and I'm not sure about the universe.
— Albert Einstein

If you are a drift-boat guide running day trips, the lunch spot is of prime importance because it offers a midday break from wading and casting exertion. No doubt each guide, or "guide-group" has a favorite lunch spot in each section of river that they regularly fish.

Back in the good old days before the Lower Deschutes became over-run with traffic, we conducted steelhead trips by drift boat in the waters paralleling the Lower Deschutes Access Road. Most of our day floats were from Beavertail Campground to Mack's Canyon. This was a very productive part of the river from mid-August until the end of October. About halfway down this nine-mile stretch across from the mouth of a huge side canyon is a riffle that stacks with steelhead because of perfect water speed and abundant cover offered by large bottom structure, but more from the fact of a large mid-river spring that emanates from an aquifer that runs down the canyon. This spring tends to keep the river cool during the hot summer and warmer than the cold fall months. In this perfect fly fishing run, the river tapers from the beach in a natural opening in the streamside vegetation on a shallow bend and the current gradually quickened as the water became deeper. Here the road runs very close to the water and a natural wide parking spot allowed our shuttle drivers to meet us for lunch. Frequently, even though the mid day sun was full on the water, clients would often hook a fish or two while the guides were fixing lunch. Of course, this fishing hole became known as the "Lunch Spot."

Years later, after this stretch was overrun by road traffic and we had long since quit trying to fish it, I met a young angler at a Fly Fishers of Oregon meeting. He mentioned that he had been fishing for the Deschutes for steelhead. I asked him if he had done any good? He replied that yes, he had caught two at the "Lunch Spot." He of course had no idea of my relationship to that piece of water. In a playful mood I asked him how he thought that water got its name? A quizzled look came over his face and he replied, "I guess that's where steelhead come to eat lunch." I agreed that he was probably right.

After the "Lunch Spot Riffle" became so popular that we abandoned the practice of eating lunch there, we started eating lunch across the river on a sand bar shaded by huge alder trees. One day after a particularly productive morning, I parked my boat in the cove downstream of the sand bar. My clients seated themselves in a couple of folding chairs. A table was set up and a barbeque was lit to cook some rib-eyes. My back was to the river and a faint sound coming from the direction of the boat caught my attention. I turned and in disbelief noted that there was another boat parked in the cove with two scruffy looking guys getting out of it. One said that they weren't fishing but wanted to set up a hunting camp on the bench above the sand bar. He asked if it was all right with us. Against my better judgement I said, "Okay." This stretch of river is all public land and although invading our lunch area would be considered bad manners by most people, there are no official guidelines for such actions.

They started hauling gear from their boat up the bank to their prospective camp sight. I went back to preparing lunch for my clients. Then one of the hunters pulls a spinning rod from the boat and using an orange Tadpolly plug, catches a steelhead right in front of my anchored boat. Landing the fish and whacking it on the head, he states that plugs will always catch more steelhead than the fly fishing gear we have in my boat, which of course raises my hackles slightly, but I ignore him and feed my clients.

Some minutes later I noticed that this person was still fishing fifty yards downstream of the boats. There was a large tree still further downstream, and he disappeared behind it. A little while later I saw a steelhead jump high in the air and the angler let out a loud taunting yell to be sure that we had seen it. Then there was silence.

We are seated eating our steaks when the other hunter comes to the table asking if I have a pair of pliers that he can borrow? I say yes, I have pliers, but they are expensive stainless steel tools, and thinking they are to be used for assembling a tent, I reply that I don't want them used for twisting any rusty bolts or the like. The hunter informs me that his partner has a hook stuck in his hand.

I offer my services and explain that I have some experience with such injuries. We entered their campsite. There was the macho spin fisherman sitting on a cooler with a bag of ice on his left hand. A 1/0 treble hook has been removed from his Tadpolly. One point is buried in the joint of his left thumb. It seemed that as he was landing a steelhead his rod was bent with the weight of the thrashing fish, and as he reached out his hand to grab the fish, the hooks came free and the load in the rod fired the hook into his hand. At the time the Deschutes was designated a single barbless hook fishery. This guy was fishing with treble hooks and the barbs weren’t crushed down. He was breaking a law that was put in place to conserve wild fish.

It was then that I lost my last little bit of patience and rage started to build. I grabbed the man by the wrist with my left hand and the hook with the pliers in my right hand. With tears streaming down his cheeks, he screamed, “No,” and tried to pull free. But I had him, and he couldn’t move without extreme pain.

Then I calmly informed him, he could let me remove the hook, or get in the boat and let his buddy row him to the landing site and then drive him to The Dalles hospital where they could remove the hook after administrating anesthetic. Both men agreed the hospital had the most appeal. They got in their boat and left. We never saw the hunters again. My clients were never aware of what happened in the hunting camp, which was out of range of their sight and hearing.

After lunch one of my clients caught a ten-pound steelhead just downstream from the tree. He asked how I was able to negotiate the water for him?

I answered that the hunters were simply hooked on quiet diplomacy.

Chapter 21

Steelhead Fly Fishing Mysteries

"Without deviation from the norm, progress is not possible."

— Frank Zappa

First appeared in Flyfishing Magazine – 1988
There have been many changes since then!

Few things are more inspiring to Northwest anglers than a box of well-worn steelhead flies--especially flies with ragged hackles, tattered bodies, or broken ribs, often with hook points of bare metal honed to surgical sharpness. The owner doesn't pack it around just to show off his tying skills. His fly box is a history of days spent searching water and sometimes successfully hooking and landing fish that make less-successful days worthwhile.

Houston Fuller and I examined a box like that several years ago on a trip to the North Umpqua River. We had spent an unsuccessful morning on water around the mouth of Steamboat Creek. Deciding to break for lunch, we climbed the trail to the Forest Service parking lot. When we had arrived earlier that morning ours had been the only car.

Now there were several, including a large station wagon where three elderly gentlemen sat on its tailgate eating lunch. On the floor behind them lay their fishing paraphernalia and a bright ten-pound steelhead. After we introduced ourselves, our conversation quickly turned to the morning's fishing and the fish in the car. Fishing had been slow all week and this was the only steelhead they had touched that morning. They had fished the Umpqua together for twenty-five years and had caught lots of steelhead. I asked the inevitable question, "What are the best fly patterns for this river?" One fellow reached around behind him and after fumbling in his vest handed me a beat-up old #90 Perrine fly box. I undid the large rubber band that held it together. It contained four dozen size four long-shank Muddler Minnows so sparsely dressed they looked like they'd been plucked. That was it. The old man said it was the only fly he and his companions used. "When they won't take a Muddler, they won't take nothin'." Some fishermen believe one fly will catch steelhead under any conditions. If that were true, would fly fishing be as much fun?

The Deschutes River occupies most of my summers. From August until late November, I work there as a professional steelhead guide. The Deschutes is a big desert river in a deep basalt canyon. The air is dry and only a narrow strip bordering the water contains much green vegetation. Head-high canary grass, horsetails, and short scrubby alders can make a nearly impenetrable wall. The Deschutes is big and strong. Its waters are always richly laden with algae giving the fish lots of cover. With water temperatures in the fifties most of the time, it is one of the world's best floating-line steelhead fisheries.

Don Wysham, Dave Bretton, and I had launched my seventeen-foot aluminum drift boat on the Deschutes River at daylight. The morning's fishing had been active. Don had landed a couple of nice steelhead on standard Deschutes patterns: one on a Skunk Fly, the other on a Mack's Canyon. An experienced Atlantic Salmon angler, Dave had landed one steelhead and lost another on a Conrad, a fly he had used successfully in Maine. The sun was high. It was time for lunch.

I anchored the boat along a small sand bar shaded by overhanging alders and set up my folding table and gas barbecue. The first gusts of an afternoon breeze showered the water with small, yellowish-green alder leaves. Dave, who would rather fish than eat, asked about the water nearby. I suggested he walk upstream one hundred yards and fish through the riffle above the boat. It had produced many steelhead over the years. Dave searched through his fly box and selected a yellow and green Cosseboom, saying it was one of the best patterns for Atlantic Salmon.

Dave left for the riffle, Don tried the water next to the boat; and I proceeded with lunch. Shortly Dave yelled from upstream. He was into a steelhead. I turned off the grill, grabbed the net, and Don and I walked upstream to join Dave. After landing the fish, a seven-pound buck, Dave said he had watched the steelhead come to the fly from a long distance.

Don and I were fishing two-fly rigs. We had each tied on a Cosseboom; mine on the dropper, Don's on the point. The three of us took seven more fish that afternoon, all on the Cosseboom. I have since fished the Cosseboom on the Deschutes many times and have caught fish, but never as many as on that day. Was it the shower of alder leaves that turned the steelhead onto the green and yellow fly? Who knows? On the west side of the Cascade Mountains, the Cosseboom is a top producer of fresh early summer steelhead when presented with a sink-tip fly line. They also like a green and blue Shamrock in large sizes, from #1 to #4/0, possibly because both patterns resemble a squid that frequents the Oregon coast much of the year.

Many of the creatures that steelhead eat during their stay in the Ocean are brightly colored. Many are fluorescent and some are phosphorescent.

Nearly all the bobber type lures used by drift fishermen are brightly colored. Fluorescent yarns and chenille have been popular with steelhead fly tyers for over twenty years, and in fluorescent orange or flame patterns are especially effective for early winter steelhead in nearly every river and under most water conditions.

Ichthyologists at Oregon's Marine Science Center believe that even after they have returned to fresh water, steelhead may retain the "search image" of nourishing marine organisms. According to Dr. W.G. Pearcy, steelhead range far out to sea, dining mostly on squid, amphipods and euphausiids. Squid make up 90% of their high seas diet, but many food organisms are pink or orangish in nature.

Ghost Shrimp or Sand Shrimp are popular bait with the monofilament crowd. If you don't believe it, just count the empty bait cartons along your favorite stretch of water. Early- run summer steelhead are especially susceptible to these critters. Several years ago, Rod Robinson, then working for Paulson Flies in Portland, Oregon, developed a respectable imitation of the sand shrimp using chenille covered with a shellback of polyethylene. Dean Finnerty, a teenager, added further refinements. What evolved is a fly pattern so lifelike it is easily recognized by fish and anglers alike: the

Finnerty Shrimp.

Summer steelhead enter fresh water sexually immature. Unlike their winter-run cousins who move up rivers quickly to spawn, summer-run steelhead tend to dawdle. They may not spawn for several months after leaving the ocean and often school at various points during their journey. One of those points is in the estuaries just after leaving the open ocean. This is a prime habitat for ghost shrimp. Steelhead, like all trout, are opportunists. They feed on what is easily available. Winter fish pass through sand-shrimp zones more quickly, having less time to key on them.

Each river spawns its own strain of steelhead that may spread to different parts of the ocean. It makes sense that not all food organisms will be found at all locations in the same population densities. As changing currents, temperatures, and depths create different environments, the species living within each will vary with their own living requirements. Each steelhead probably eats from a slightly different menu. This might explain why fly patterns vary from river to river and why a profusion of successful patterns exists. The angler who can match what a particular strain of steelhead feeds on in the ocean might catch more steelhead. The problem is how to observe steelhead out at sea.

Both summer and winter steelhead feed, to a certain extent, in fresh water. This does not mean all fish feed actively, but that most will capitalize on situations where food is easily obtained. All steelhead are fortified with enough accumulated fat to sustain them for their entire fresh-water journey. Some strains can live for months without digesting anything. Yet, I have caught both summer and winter steelhead that have been dining on what was available to them. About twenty percent of the fish killed over the last twenty years contained remains of some freshwater organism. One male winter steelhead had just consumed fifty-four eyed salmon eggs, no doubt washed from the riverbed during high flows. Other fish have contained small nymphs, sculpins, leeches, and terrestrial insects. Beached after a heavy rain, one steelhead contained six black and yellow millipedes.

On the waters I fish there are definite periods when flies that resemble freshwater insects out-produce flies fashioned after marine organisms. This often occurs during periods of low flows when fish are pooled up. At these times, small dull-colored flies sunk to the fish's holding level can be very productive.

Jim Teeny, of Gresham, Oregon, has spent years developing methods and tackle that are the best I've seen for taking pooled fish. His fly, the

Teeny Nymph, is simply constructed from ringneck pheasant tail fibers bleached or dyed various shades of buggy-looking colors. The new "Teeny Taper" shooting head fly lines are the best available to a fly angler for getting any fly deep. Jim uses his specially constructed polarized glasses and casts only to fish he can see. This way, he can place the fly closer to the fish. Teeny Nymphs do not exactly imitate any specific insect but can resemble stonefly or mayfly nymphs or caddis larva.

Steelhead will eat the roe of any fish spawning in their area, including eggs of their own kind. When Chinook, Coho, or steelhead are spawning, many eggs are lost to the whims of currents. These periods can provide the most available food source in an otherwise nearly barren stream. At these times, an egg fly or Glo Bug can be the best producer. Glo Bugs are small spherical-shaped tufts of special yarn attached to short-shank hooks. When drifted along the bottom. they absorb water and become translucent like a natural egg.

No doubt drifting the bottom is a productive way to catch summer steelhead, but they take flies on or near the surface more often than some experienced anglers believe.

Water level may be as important to triggering surface activity as water temperature. During the first two weeks in June, 1984, on the Salmon River, an upper Sandy River tributary, I hooked nineteen steelhead on large, dark Greased Liners fished on the surface with a riffle hitch. The water ran an almost constant 47°, and was medium-high but clear, and fish were spread out through its riffles, as the water dropped, fish congregated in deeper pools for cover. These pools are hit so hard by angling pressure that the fish quickly become jaded. When the water rose with each summer rain, the steelhead would move about in the river again positioning themselves in the riffles and becoming more active. When fall rains came, the fish again sought riffles, and surface activity was consistent for a month, though the water temperature ran 41° to 42°. When water rose with the torrential rains of winter, all surface activity stopped.

I am unconvinced that every steelhead strike is about food. Steelhead can be territorial. There is a long riffle on the Salmon River where the flow deepens at the outlet of a large spring. During periods of warm weather, steelhead congregate there amid a jumble of current-breaking boulders and cool water. The surface is misleading. Viewed from the shallow side of the river many of these boulders appear only three feet deep when the spaces between them vary down to six. Conflicting currents ruffle the surface enough to conceal any fish stationed there. On the deep side of the river, a large, rotten stump surrounded by thick brush and berry vines on a high, steep bank makes a perfect blind from which to observe the entire riffle. Since few people take the time and trouble to walk this side of the river, fish remain relatively hidden from most viewers.

A doctor from Portland had hired me to teach him and his wife how to catch steelhead on a fly. It was my very first paid guide trip. The doctor had demonstrated he could control his fly line well enough from the shallow side of the river, and I had crossed the river to peek over the top of the stump with my polarized glasses. About six average-sized steelhead were clearly visible scattered through deeper water in the middle of the riffle. It looked like some of the best holding spots were in deeper water near the main current. The steelhead were constantly changing positions and bumping any fish that held in this area. I watched fascinated as these fish continued to vie for this treasured spot, ignoring the doctor's fly, also visible in the clear water. The doctor followed my instructions for placing the fly, so it covered each fish in turn, but they were so caught up in territorial competition only one fish briefly acknowledged the fly with a slap of its tail.

So engrossing was this display, I almost didn't see the largest fish holding in a narrow deep slot no more than six feet from the bank, and right below my feet. A tall, slim boulder protruded from the center of the slot like a vertical pillar. The fish, a buck with red cheeks, was holding about eighteen inches off the bottom. His caudal fin resting against the front of the pillar helped him remain so still the gray of his back blended perfectly with the river's bottom. The main force of the current ran straight down the slot and through the fish's gills, riffling the water surface and adding concealment. Only when a slick passed over the fish was I able to glimpse the white flash of his mouth as he breathed. And only luck had revealed his cover. In the whole several hundred square yards of holding water, this spot was premium. The fish holding there was at least twice as large as others in the riffle, the master of his territory. No other fish dared challenge him.

I yelled across the river to the doctor and described what I was seeing and how to present the fly. He followed my instructions. The fly fell through the water's surface upstream from the fish and entered the slot on course with the steelhead's nose. When it had drifted within three feet, the fish stiffened. Its fins swung out and became rigid. In a short, savage rush he crushed the fly and forcefully ejected it before the doctor struck. The fly sped from the fish as if frightened. I was stunned. It took me several seconds to understand what had just happened. The take had been forceful, but slack in the drifting line had absorbed it. The doctor had felt nothing. No subsequent casts persuaded this fish to strike again. It had established its dominance, and a chance at the largest fish of the season had been lost.

Many steelhead don't feed while in fresh water. What flies to use, what steelhead eat in salt or fresh water, and whether they strike to eat or dominate, there are no mysteries as to why we fish for them. They are strong, challenging, and beautiful.

Keen angler and hook designer Alec Jackson once told me that fly fishing for steelhead was tempting the unfeedable with the inedible. I might add that sport is also about understanding the unfathomable.

Chapter 22

Once Upon an October Day A story about discovery.

"If you wish to make an apple pie truly from scratch, you must first invent the universe."

—Carl Sagan

First appeared in Trout Magazine (1990?)
There have been many changes since then!

Beneath a close blanket of leaden clouds, a cold mist fell cleansing and nourishing. Leaves and stems glistened with droplets. Wreaths of white fog rose in ever-changing shapes from vegetation on the canyon floor and hovered between yellow maples and dark hemlock ridges before ascending to the inclement sky. I was wading toward a moss-covered, huge broadleaf maple spreading its gnarled limbs over a stretch where rapids lost their momentum and became a pool. The maple's canopy of bright yellow leaves gave the river an amber hue; moisture on the maple's leaves trickled down their veins to form miniature streams falling as diamond droplets to the river's pool. From its pools — a kaleidoscope of earth tones — an invisible flow of nutrients had triggered the last algae bloom of the year. There had been no winter flows to scrub it free.

The river wound through a violent volcanic terrain where untidy pyroclastic flows had once deposited ash and globs of hot magma over solidified lava. Dominated by the huge maple, the pool's perimeter at one time had been molten. Now it was a ledge of hard brown basalt. As water slowed in the pool, the rocks in its bottom became smaller and smaller until the bed of the deepest part and tail-out was a size steelhead like to spawn in. But that wouldn't be for a couple of months, after the most violent winter storms. Nowhere in the pool had sand collected… the current was too swift.

Wading was slow and treacherous, impossible without a staff. I stepped on top of a larger-than-average boulder to gain elevation, scanning with my Polaroids, straining to search water already fished. Were they there, those gray ghosts among the tan boulders? No steelhead were in sight.

The mist stopped for a moment. I slid back the hood of my Gortex wading jacket, fumbled in the breast pocket of my wool shirt for a cigarette and matches. Lighting up, I surveyed the water downstream; it seemed almost too slow and flat to hold fish. It was late October. The crowds from town were gone, leaving the river to those who lived along its banks. How relaxing! Not another person in sight.

I shot my floating line and dropped a big black-and-green fly close to the brown ledge. My 10-foot graphite rod easily swung the belly of the double taper upstream and the rod's tiptop followed the fly as it swam in an arc across the river. My line was freshly dressed and rode the undulating surface tension perfectly. I had made the cast to contrast the fly's speed with the current's speed. It hung barely submerged in the fast water and slowly crawled across the river until the bend in the line reversed itself and pulled the fly into the slower part of the pool directly below me.

The take was almost… nonchalant: first a gentle straightening of the slack in the line, then tension increased, bending the rod down to the handle as the fish took the fly from the rear and lazily turned back to its lie. My adrenalin surged. I swung the rod horizontally toward the bank behind me and struck, driving the barbless hook into the hinge of the fish's mouth. In a shower of spray, its wide tail broke the surface. The first run took all my fly line and some of the white braided backing as I floundered toward shore.

The fish stopped just short of the rapids below the pool and shook its head as I slung my wading staff over my shoulder. Steady pressure from the big rod worked the fish back to the pool's center. The battle was strong and lengthy but not showy, and after a while, I slid the fish on its side into a shallow pool between some boulders to photograph her against a background of submerged dead leaves, a female about seven pounds. Her adipose fin was missing, exposing her hatchery origin. She was lean and rose-colored from a long stay in freshwater. Thick red filaments showed through a triangular notch in her right gill plate, evidence of a previous injury. Despite this, she was still healthy and capable of spawning. The hook came easily from her mouth. I grasped her by the tail, slid her into the river, revived her, then watched her melt into the depths across the pool. And after securing my bedraggled fly in the hook-keeper, watched the wreaths of fog hanging over the wide canyon. The air was suddenly fresher, the firs and hemlocks greener, the river less mysterious. I stood watching the river for a long time before finally wading toward deeper water at the center of the pool to peer into a channel by the brown ledge. Several long gray shapes hung suspended in the flow. Backing quietly from the pool, I left them in peace — it was enough to know they were there.

The trail from the river was steep. It led me under dripping cedar boughs, through a tangle of vine maple, a carpet of shamrocks, and finally across a narrow bridge. Hiking upstream divulged an old friend busily tending his yard. We chatted about fishing, and he told me about his 14-year-old son's first steelhead before I continued upstream for another quarter of a mile to a long flat pool with a fast deep slot at the head. Several steelhead were holding under some long, trailing vine maple branches on the opposite side of the fast water, effectively screened from any presentation of a fly. After a dozen casts, my fly hung in one of the branches, and I broke it off. The experience encouraged me to give up on those fish and work my way down the pool in search of others.

Cast after cast, I threw my fly to the opposite bank, mending line upstream with enough slack to drift with the speed of the current and, as the line tightened at the end of the swing, mend it toward the near bank. The fly would change direction and speed up slightly as it swam through the calm water directly below me. I had covered about fifty yards of premium water and was beginning to think my first fish was all this day had to offer. My thoughts began to drift from fishing to business, to family, to… interrupted by a wrenching pull as a heavy fish turned and caught the fly as it swam into slack water. I had been casting mechanically with the line pinched tightly to the cork of my rod handle with my index finger. Now smoke hung in the air as the friction of the fast-moving line burned my finger, a product of our mutually surprised reactions instantaneous and brutal as 12 to 14 pounds of bright steelhead erupted through the surface in a great cartwheeling leap.

Again and again, the big steelhead tore the river's placid surface in plumes of spray, racing downstream against my tightly set drag and bending the rod to its handle. I placed its short extension butt against my belly and slid my hand onto the bare blank for more leverage. The hook keeper dug into my ring finger, and the spinning handle barked my knuckles as I palmed the reel. My backing's bright red 50-yard mark shot through the rod guides and hung over the water. The fish stopped briefly at the tail of the pool, then turned and bolted back toward me. Frantically cranking to reel in slack I barely regained line fast enough to maintain tension. The fish stalled and sulked half a line's length below me. I increased pressure, afraid to let it regain lost energy. Suddenly flashes and boils erupted as the fish reacted, rolling end over end beneath the surface, shaking its head violently.

There was the feeling of grating as the fly tore from the flesh. The line went slack. The surface of the pool was quiet again. The falling mist absorbed the river's music. All was calm. I stood in the margin of the pool, clear water flowing around me, surrounded by deep greens, autumn yellows, and gray mist, my bright yellow fly line slack and trailing in the flow. Though motionless as a heron, my body was electric, my mind racing to comprehend such violence in such a serene setting. After reeling in my line and checking the leader and fly, I waded to the bank.

Downstream, the river divided into three channels around two islands. At the head of the far channel was a holding spot next to some overhanging salmonberry bushes and alder trees. It was a small pool, no more than twenty feet wide and forty feet long. On my fourth cast, there was a gentle take, like this morning's first, just after the fly had changed direction. I drove the hook home once the full weight of the fish was felt. An average-sized, red-colored male steelhead rolled and flopped on the surface twice before tearing out of the tiny pool downstream into steep and narrow rapids with tightly spaced tall-standing waves. It ended in a deep round pool with a truck-sized, pillar-shaped boulder protruding from its center. The pool lay in the elbow of a right-angle bend. The island I stood on was thickly covered with head-high willows and a huge log jam on the downstream end. End over end the fish tumbled through the entire length of the rapids so quickly it left me standing on one end of the island while it was already at the other, my fly line and backing strung through the willows and disappearing around the log jam. On large slick boulders, I fought my way through the willows, tripping twice on my wading staff before slinging it over my shoulder to get things under control.

The fish was still taking line somewhere around the bend. I stopped crashing through the brush briefly and hauled back on the rod, straining the leader near its breaking point. The fish stopped, giving me the ability to reel my way down to it. Approaching the clear pool, I could see the fish's tail working as it tried to swim behind the giant boulder. Wading below, I steered it back to my side of the river, where it fought long and doggedly. Each time I pressured the fish to within five feet of the gravel at my feet, it would take twenty feet of line. For five minutes we seesawed back and forth, the fish constantly in view before it finally tired, allowing it to be beached. The eight-pound male was still fat and fresh, but already mature, with deep crimson flanks and gill covers, the fly firmly embedded in its hooked lower jaw. I removed it and eased the fish into the current. Wrenching free of my grasp it steamed off into the deep water in a final show of defiance. I rested briefly on the island, watching a pine squirrel busily storing cones for the winter. Below the pool, patches of gravel had been swept clean by spawning Chinook salmon. A huge carcass lay half-in, half-out of the water, its mission accomplished.

Wading downstream, I methodically worked the whole river for several hundred yards without a touch though three steelhead had been hooked in less than two hours of fishing. There had been a consistent pattern to the water the fish held in and definite similarities in the way the fly had been working when each strike occurred. In my almost twenty years of fishing, these were not my first steelhead with a greased line, but one thing *was* different: the water was cold; 41 degrees according to my dial thermometer. I had never taken steelhead near the surface in water anywhere near that cold, nor imagined it could be done. This was something new.

My curiosity aroused, I fished on downstream, searching for a patch of water with that special look, where currents converge at just the right speed over the right depth. It took several minutes to find what I was looking for. The fly line, not the water's surface, had brought it to my attention. I had cast and mended as usual to the opposite bank across what seemed water too fast and broken. The line bent out of the fast current and hung the fly momentarily in an unnoticed calm spot in the center of the river before a faster current pulled slack out of my line and the fly changed direction. My fly reached perfect speed as it coasted through the slick.

I knew what was coming before feeling the fish's solid, decisive yank.

This steelhead was a female, bright and fresh from the ocean. Cold white and silver flashed from her belly and flanks as she turned and twisted beneath the surface before shattering it with a jump. It was my first winter steelhead of the season, hard and mean, the leading edges of her glassy lower fins milky white, and the demarcation on her flanks razor-sharp and straight, gunmetal gray on top and silver below. She had probably been swimming continually upstream against hard current since she had left the sea four days ago. The headlong race to the mountains had momentarily drained her strength. She was 150 miles from the salt. "Nickel bright" the local folks call them. She was native, and wild and weighed about six pounds.

I cradled her gently in the shallows and photographed this beautiful metallic fish suspended in clear cold water over finely porous basalt gravel. She revived slowly. It was 15 minutes until she fully recovered, my bare hands numb from holding her in the frigid water. Finally, she surged into the current and hugged the bottom as she sought the covering depth of midstream.

The mist still fell. The sun was low and the temperature dropping. Evening had arrived unnoticed during the heat of battle. A water ouzel landed on a moss-covered boulder, under drooping hemlock branches on the opposite bank. It teetered and cocked its head, surveying me with a beady eye, and diving several times into a tiny pool before it fluttered off downstream from whence it had come. I stood quietly thinking and listening to the river's music. Feeling relaxed and alive, letting its sound penetrate my being and run through my soul. Though originally out here for entertainment, much more was found: a window into the unknown. I sat down on a large wet boulder in the middle of the barren gravel bar and stared at the spot where the fish had taken the fly. It was an obvious lie in the center of what seemed the best migration route, just room enough for one fish. How long had this fish rested there before I had come downstream to meet it? I only knew that the river needed her as she needed the river. They were a part of each other.

Why had she taken the fly? Nearly everything I had read told me that winter steelhead never rise to the surface to take a fly. Many people feel that even summer steelhead don't rise often when the water temperature falls below 50 degrees. Water temperatures in the low 40s normally require sinking lines or drift tackle. I wondered if for many years I had missed out on some great fishing.

Then checking my watch; there was enough

time left to fish one more piece of water before dark. Below me the river ran through a short stretch of boulder-filled rapids and then fanned out, forming a wide, gentle riffle. There would be steelhead there. I had caught many there in the past using a sink tip line. Would they rise to the surface if the fly was presented right?

I hurried across the river and started casting at the head of the riffle. It was a graceful piece of water, nearly flat, with uniform flow from bank to bank. It reached a depth of almost six feet at its center, with its surface so smooth it looked much shallower. A few oil drum-sized boulders in the flow added to this illusion. Few people fished this water that looked too shallow. Downstream, the bridge stood, ghostly in the mist. Between the bridge and where I stood the river turned lead gray, and mist was rising from it. The air had become cooler than the river. The sky was clearing — it would freeze tonight.

I cast quartering downstream, letting the river push on the belly of the line and speed the fly slightly as it swept an inch below the surface. Concentrated on duplicating the speed and course of the fly the previous fish had taken, knowing if I presented the fly to exactly the right angle across the current little mending was necessary. With the bright-colored fly line, it was easy. The strike came almost immediately. I lowered my rod tip and allowed the fish to turn and hook himself, an eight-pound buck with silver sides and ruby gill plates. It, too, was a winter fish. It fought long and hard before being landed, admired, and released.

I re-waded the river and reached my van just before dark. While packing my gear, my mind analyzed the afternoon. Never before, on this difficult river, had I been so successful with a floating line. Five steelhead hooked in about three hours of fishing was a good day with any kind of gear. However, with a floating line, it seemed impossible. Each fish had entered the river at a different time of the year, yet each had struck the same fly. In his book *Greased Line Fishing for Salmon,* A.H.E. Wood has argued that presentation, rather than fly pattern, matters most. I had read but never fully understood this. I thought back to conversations I'd had over the years with Bill McMillan and Bill Bakke and realized that 15 years ago they had been catching fish by this method.

Each fish had been a jewel unto itself. Each had taught me something and each had delighted me. Below the van, in gathering darkness, the river slid noisily toward the sea. Today she had pulled back her veil and revealed a secret or two. Flowing around me she had cleansed a few anxieties of the civilized world from my mind. It was time to head home.

Chapter 23

The Evolution of Big Black

"Nature is pleased with simplicity. And nature is no dummy."
— Isaac Newton

Reprinted from Fly Fisherman Magazine, 1996
There have been many changes since then!

The air has that balmy crispness of early spring that permeates the soul with the heady smells of cotton wood and alder leaves half grown from buds dripping the resins of rebirth. Nature is a kaleidoscope of green radiating from the canyon. The trees, the water, even the lightly leaden sky seems slightly green. A steady overnight rain has removed the last lingering impurities from the atmosphere. Now, the air is starkly clear. Wreaths of white fog hung suspended between ramparts cloaked in giant Douglas Fir trees. The water is at the perfect level and clarity for steelhead fishing. With great expectations Chuck, Stens and I launch the drift boat. He rows. Chuck and I gaze from the front seat in silence overpowered by the smells, temperatures, textures, and colors of the canyon. We drift down the river a while and leave the boat anchored at the upstream tip of an island. Chuck and

Stens survey the wide tail-out. There isn't room for three, so I chose the smaller back channel. Here the river is a lower gradient with soft currents and medium depth. The type IV sinking tip section of my line is replaced with a type II. A simple two and a half inch long, unweighted Black Steelhead Bunny is attached to the end of the arm length stout leader.

The water has dropped so much in the past twenty four hours that the first run is too shallow. I cross the river to fish the next run from the opposite shore. Here a couple of mid- stream boulders break the current and form a perfectly textured riffle. The first cast is short, with barely enough line to load the tip of my fifteen foot rod. The fly lands broad side to the current and the rod gradually rotates downstream to keep it that way for as long as possible. The fly slowly speeds up through the swing....nothing. The next cast is extended two feet....same swing nothing. The fly line is lengthened another three feet so that the riffle is

covered in concentric arcs. The fly drifts five feet under light tension, then the line begins to slowly tighten. I hold my breath as the pressure increases to the point where the fish can be felt swimming on the other end of the line. The rod tip is moved down stream. With this added pressure the fish bolts directly away and sets the hook deeply into the hinge muscle of her mouth. The battle, though strong and dramatic, is short lived and ends as Stens brings Chuck and the drift boat down to me. Of course, we have to take pictures and yahoo a little. The prize is a perfectly formed seven pound, wild, chromer hen steelhead. She is held long enough to regain her strength and is returned to the currents. Chuck examines the now slimy fly. "It's big....looks pretty simple why did you select this one?"

I drop the fly into the shallow water between us and it comes alive with graceful motion, inky-black and glistening silver. It is subtle but very apparent against the grayish river bottom.

Stens, who has been uncustomarily quiet, drops his fly into the water next to mine. It sinks headfirst swiftly to the bottom. The flies are identical except his has small nickel plated lead eyes. His fly rests lightly on the bottom in the gentle current and breathes and wiggles like a tiny streamer of jet black smoke.

"It looks pretty convincing", says Chuck. "What do you call it?"

Stens and I look at each other. "We call it Big Black", is the dual reply.

This may be one of the all-time deadliest fly patterns for spring and early summer steelhead. For the past three spring seasons it has accounted for about eighty percent of my catch. I fish a river that has a nearly continuous year around run of steelhead. From late March through May, bright winter run fish will be mixed with early summers. The Big Black Fly is equally effective on both.

Many popular northwest steelhead patterns are predominantly black. Black is easily seen in many different water and light conditions and has the most distinguishable silhouette. Black is a color that doesn't readily spook fish even when a fly is presented in a large size. Rabbit fur is a material that comes alive when fully saturated and suspended in water. Every fiber is in motion and pulsates with life. Most strikes result in the fish being hooked deep in the mouth, which would lead to the conclusion that the prey was intended to be swallowed. This might indicate that the Big Black mimics some food source such as squid or out migrating juvenile lampreys. But then maybe, it's just a big black obnoxious critter invading their space It works.

Big Black seems to be most productive if presented near the bottom and broad side to the fish. We call it a deep greased line presentation. The cast is made across the current and slightly upstream. A small mend then places the line perpendicular to the current flow with the rod in an upstream position.

The rod is then rotated downstream with the speed of the current so that the fly line lays across the current until the fly comes under light tension. The rod tip leads the fly line downstream slowly until both rod and line are parallel with the current. The fly crawls along the bottom of the river remaining broad side to the flow through much of the swing until it stops directly below the angler. Then the angler steps down stream and the process is repeated until the whole run is systematically covered. Having a fly pattern that you know will catch fish is a distinct advantage. Problems get easier when you can eliminate some of the variables. When you know you have a dependable fly, then you can concentrate all your energy on finding fish. A lot of time can be used up in the decision making of which fly to tie on. More time may be squandered worrying if the right color has been selected rather than if the fly is fishing at the right depth and speed. Fly speed and depth are everything. The right presentation is worth more than a box containing a hundred different fly patterns.

To be able to fish confidently at depth around large cover, you must have no emotional attachment to the fly. If the fly becomes snagged, it must be broken off without pangs of material loss. Only then will the angler be able to fish most effectively in the places that hold the maximum numbers of steelhead. It makes sense to fish flies that are quick and easy to tie. The fastest flies to tie are the ones that incorporate the fewest kinds of materials. Steelhead Bunnies are some of the easiest.

More often than not the angler is equipped with a lot of pretty flies in varying colors, but which are all of the same sink rate. Usually, the artistic nature of the fly-tying angler demands that steelhead must surely be more easily enticed with the most complex fly designs. These artsy flies take a lot of time to tie. The angler is not prone to fish these flies at risk.

Steelhead are notoriously fickle and love to change holds with changes of water level and temperature. Some days a lot of different water types might be explored just to find the fish. Steelhead will rest and travel in depths from one to ten feet deep. The closer the fly is to the fish the more often it will draw strikes. Obviously having flies which are designed to function efficiently at these differing depths can be a distinct asset. Lead eyes or brass beads of differing weights may be tied into these flies so that the angler is more easily adaptable to changing conditions.

The first big black rabbit strip fly I ever saw was a copy of one attributed to Mel Krieger. It was a three inch long narrow strip of black rabbit pelt tied on a standard looped eye salmon hook. Close to the eye of the hook were attached a pair of black painted medium size lead eyes. I tried fishing that fly on the Salmon River near my home and immediately hooked steelhead and chinooks with it. It was deadly in several sizes and weights but had a nasty habit of becoming tangled. The tail would often irritatingly wrap around the hook while casting. This was especially true in the sizes which were proving to be most effective. The answer came from a group of astute, young Alaskan guides who spend their winter seasons fishing steelhead on the rivers which drain the northern Cascades in Washington State.

Steve Kruse stopped by on his way back from a multi-day trip on the Skykomish River where he had been fishing with Ed Ward and Deck Hogan. Steve was sporting the big grin of a successful hunt.

"How'd ya' do", I asked?

“It was great," Steve said as he slid into a chair on the other side of my fly tying table. " Got one fish each day, the smallest eleven, the largest fourteen pounds. The Sky is a beautiful river, endless riffles. The fish are strong real strong". Then he took me on a vicarious trip

complete with screaming reels and leaping chrome plated fish and bald eagles and shared comradeship.

All the while the story unfolded, I was eyeing the unusually large, bright scarlet fly stuck in the braid on his battered baseball cap. It appeared to be a three inch long, all red bunny bugger tied on a 2/0 looped eye salmon hook.

"Oh this", he replied as he took the fly from his hat and handed it to me, "they call it Big Red. It's the hottest thing on the Sky."

It was a sparse tied bunny bugger with the narrow rabbit strip palmered between ribs of wide pearl mylar. I made a mental image of the fly. The tail was one half inch long. There were four wraps of mylar and rabbit over a thin body of scarlet dubbing. The fly was sleek, snaky, and apparently foul proof.

Kruse no sooner left than I was splitting down some red rabbit strips with a razor blade and a half dozen Big Reds were tied. Never caring much for large irons because of the hook setting problems they cause, nickel plated ring eye streamer hooks were selected. Then my attention turned to other colors of rabbit pelt. Several purple and then black ones were added to the collection. The pearl rib didn't look right on the black fly, so it was changed to silver.

The next morning found me on a favorite piece of water on a local steelhead river. Naturally, a Big

Red was my starting fly, but it hung on the bottom and broke off halfway through the sweet spot in the run. When I opened my fly box, the black version of the fly seemed dominant in the early light. Since this piece of water is small, it was easily fished again. For the effort of twenty casts my reward was a pair of nice winter steelhead. One was landed, the other came off at the beach.

That fly was named after Big Red and became known locally as Big Black. Since then, the Big Black has gone through several small modifications. A very lightweight version tied on a size 1.5 Alec Jackson nickel plated spey hook and a silver bead head version for fishing slightly deeper water. Both flies lack body and rib as gaps are left between the turns of rabbit strip to let the silver hook show through. One style consists of a rabbit strip and a hook and the other is a rabbit strip, a bead, and a hook. I have always felt that the best engineering incorporates the fewest parts possible that will achieve the desired result. I would rather fish than tie and would rather have a sacrificial volume of flies than a few fancy ones. The Big Black Fly has been most successful in lengths around two and a half inches, on the rivers that I fish. But it is tied in sizes up to eight inches long. These large flies can be very effective in rivers which contain really large steelhead or where steelhead have been pooled for a long period of time.

It is most economical to buy full hides and cut your own strips. Most commercial cut strips are cut in widths appropriate for Zonkers which are too wide for good bunnies. Hides should be picked carefully. Rabbit strips cut from prime pelts with long guard hares provide the best loft which in turn contributes to the most movement of individual fibers when fully saturated. A thin, but strong supple hide is desirable for ease of tying. Avoid thick, soft, puffy leather as it tends to roll while palmering and the bulk makes tying a small, efficient head nearly impossible.

As the fly changes size, it must also change form to remain effective at hooking. Large hooks take more force to penetrate than do small hooks, because of their larger frontal area. Large hooks create more water drag while casting and are also more injurious to the fish. This is no problem when tying a two and a half inch long fly as hooks are easily obtainable which fit both the fly and the fish. Problems, however, do arise when tying flies larger than this.

The fly will tail wrap if the leather of the rabbit strip extends more than one quarter of an inch beyond the bend of the hook. That is unless some device is installed to prevent it from doing so. The hook must be positioned so that the fish will be fairly and securely hooked when it takes the fly. This pretty much dictates that the hook be near the rear of the fly. Long flies should be flexible to retain their maximum movement in the water. This criterion has resulted in some interesting fly-tying innovations.

Bead Head Big Black

Hook: TMC 9394, #2 - #6

Head: 3/16" nickel plated brass bead

Thread: black flat waxed Wing: Black Rabbit Zonker Strip

Lay down a dozen wraps of tying thread directly above the hook point on the hook shank. Coat these wraps liberally with Flexament. A narrow cut strip of black rabbit pelt is attached to this wet foundation with several more wraps of thread. The thread is moved to the eye of the hook with four equally spaced wraps. Then the rabbit is palmered to cover the thread on the bare hook shank. An extra wrap of rabbit strip behind the bead completes the fly.

The rabbit strip tends to foul if the leather is allowed to extend more than on quarter of an inch beyond the tie in point. This approach builds a two- and one-half inch fly on a #2 TMC 9394 hook. Non - fouling flies with longer tails are tied by installing a horizontal loop of forty-pound monofilament at the tie in point before the rabbit strip is attached. This loop should be about one-half inch long and at least a quarter of an inch wide.

Unweighted Big Black

Same fly, leave out the bead. The lighter the hook the more action the fly will have. Alec Jackson Spey hooks are best and come in five colors including nickel and gold.

When this was first published in 1996, before the popularity of Intruder flies, 2.5" was considered a big fly. Now steelhead flies of 2.5" to 4" are common. Spey rods in the 1990's 14' to 15' 9/10 weight were commonly used for steelhead. Since then, there has been a vast evolution in fly lines that enable anglers to cast larger flies with lighter rods. Unfortunately, as this paragraph is being written in the last days of 2022, steelhead runs have declined, and we no longer have the prolific year around runs written about in this chapter.

As Henry Ford said, "You can have any color you want as long as its black." *This was the last sentence in the Fly Fisherman article.* Fact is Steelhead have been caught on many colors of Bunny Leaches, including black, purple, olive, red, pink, and orange.

Chapter 24

Belize, In Search of the Golden Fleece

"There is a pleasure in the pathless woods, there is a rapture on the lonely shore, there is a society where none intrudes, by the sea and the music in its roar."

—Lord Byron

A bronze-rimmed, fluffy cloud hangs low on the horizon. It masks the face of the late afternoon fire-ball tropical sun. Long, narrow beams of sterling sunlight move unevenly from behind the slowly changing shape of the cloud as it floats across the sky. The soft warm air cools slightly. The faintest zephyr turns the surface of the coastal lagoon to hammered gold. The lagoon is surrounded by huge, lush jade green mangroves. The trim white and aqua skiff glides slowly in the silent panorama; sliding with its gilded reflection across the shallow water. Only the soft swish of Derrick's push pole breaks the primordial silence. The scent of wet mangrove roots and salt marsh permeates the air with soft, sulphur musk. All is held in the inverted bowl of a slowly darkening turquoise sky. Silver, gold, bronze, turquoise and jade w e are as time travelers afloat in a land known well to the ancient Maya.

Jim, Patty, and I have returned to southern Belize for our second trip. We are searching for Permit. Permits are beautiful, incredibly alert, cautious fish that inhabit many shallow waters ringing the Caribbean Sea. They have long been the "Golden Fleece" for saltwater fly anglers and have a reputation for being one of the most difficult shallow water fish to take with a fly. We are halfway through our second ten day trip to Belize and although we have fished with a number of different guides and cast to dozens, only Patty has even hooked a Permit, which quickly broke her off. We are becoming intimidated. The pressure is on.

Four days ago, we were at a Lodge in Placencia, Belize but had a disagreement with the crooked owner about billing and left to find another hotel. The last day at the lodge, Derek Muschamp was our guide. But when we left, he did too and became self-employed, so we hired him to help us catch permit. Yesterday Derrick had caught a couple brownish gray crabs that Permit feed on in the mud bottom lagoons. We put them in water in the bottom of a coffee can and took them to the hotel.

I had brought a sizable fly tying kit with me. Last night I had stayed up until midnight using these crabs as models and with materials available in my kit a new fly was developed. I had tied four of them. First, I fashioned several size 1/0 Mustad stainless steel hooks into keel fly hooks. Then I wrapped the shanks with heavy lead wire. Next, I cut several #9 rubber bands and dotted them with a felt marker. These were secured to the side of the hook shank, over the lead wire. They looked like legs and claws. Alternating bundles of natural and dyed brown deer hair were tied-on next and trimmed to match the shape of a crab carapace. The body fits inside of the bend of the hook so that the hook would ride with the point on top of the fly.

When I showed the flies to Derrick he said simply, "Mumm, nice job. I know a place where these will work. I will take you there."

He has brought us to this huge lagoon by way of hidden channels. We traveled several miles from the coast through a maze of mangrove swamps. It is one of his secret spots. He assures us that no one has fished here for months.

This and other inter-connecting saltwater lakes cover thousands of acres and are protected from the prevailing Caribbean wind. Subject to tidal influence, the currents are very soft as is the bottom, which is composed of brown silts which have collected here for thousands of years. Mostly hidden from the eye, life teems in this warm, shallow, nutrient rich water. Tiny crabs and shrimp burrow into the bottom ooze and hide from patrolling Permit, Bonefish and Jack Crevalle.

Hundreds of yards in front of the boat, a sparsely vegetated peninsula protrudes from the shore, forming a wind shadow in a tiny bay. In the bay something moves the apparition of a fish or an errant wave breaking gently on a shallow bar? Minutes pass we silently strain to see in the

distant glare.

Derrick speaks softly and points, "Permit...one hundred yards...eleven o'clock just beyond that little mangrove point he's turning left, coming out of that bay".

Standing high on the bow platform with rod firmly in hand, something deep inside me says, "Yes, I know!" The springs inside my muscles tightened and the pain is gone from my sun baked eyes.

Derrick poles the boat steadily closer. We are still fifty yards away from the peninsula when a long thin black dorsal fin appears as the fish feeds erratically along the edge of the wind shadow. Suddenly, there is a huge boil and the Permit bolts for deeper water. Even though we are still far away,

I think he has seen us.

Derrick's soft quiet voice consoles me. "Mm .... Something' spooked that Permit, Mon. But it couldn't have been us. We are too far away."

Moments later the Permit reappears twenty yards in front of the boat, his wake turning toward us. He comes at us so fast; I barely have enough time to false cast enough line to load the ten weight rod. The fly lands four feet directly in front of the fish. Allowing several seconds for the fly to sink to the bottom, Derrick shouts, "Strip, strip". I move the line with two quick four inch strips. The fish accelerates and inhales the fly. I pull in the slack and the line tightens. I yank but feel nothing and pull the fly away from the fish as he charges about looking for it and then cruises past the boat, beyond our reach.

Derrick expertly turns the boat end for end, and poling vigorously, gives pursuit. The Permit cruises fast along the edge of the mangroves and into water so shallow that it lies over on its side several times to get passage.

Derrick proclaims, "That is a nice fish!"

Finally, the boat is in a close position again. I have to cast quartering into the wind with the line and fly crossing the center of the boat...which is filled with people. It is a tricky, unnerving presentation. The cast lands short. I strip line frantically, trying to pull the heavy fly line out of the water to make another cast. Derrick poles the boat hard, keeping pace with the fast moving fish. Surprisingly, it has not spooked. I take a deep breath and let my nerves settle. Shooting line on the back cast and hauling hard on the forward cast, my body arches forward and drives the narrow loop into the wind. The bulky fly lands quietly four feet in front of and slightly beyond the moving fish. I count to four and twitch the fly. The Permit sees it and strikes. I feel him pull. Nothing! (Expletive deleted.)

He spins around twice in the knee-deep water thirty feet from the boat where the light gives us a glare-free view of his desperate effort to locate the fly. Vortices of muddy water whirl up with each kick of his wide black tail as he maneuvers to find the fly. I twitch the fly again. Somehow, he spots the fly in all this mess, probably by feel, and charges, but loses sight of it in a plume of mud and misses. I keep stripping the fly with the Permit in hot pursuit, his long, thin, black dorsal fin slicing through his bulging bow wake. I feel the grab and make a hard two-foot strip with my left hand. The line comes tight as the sharp stainless steel hook bites deep into his fleshy mouth. There is a wild thrashing at the end of my line.

"You've got him!" Derrick yells. "Get the slack line clear...get him on the reel cause all hell is going to break loose! You've got him. God, I love you for that mon!"

There is a cheer from Jim and Patty. I am hooked to my first Permit and don't have the faintest idea what to expect. Adrenaline pumps through my already over-crowded veins. At first the fish doesn't do much. For a few seconds he doesn't realize he is hooked. He just wallows around making big bulges and kicking up plumes of spray with his wide vee-shaped black tail. This gives me precious time to get organized. I set the hook again with confidence. The Permit takes fifty yards of backing at moderate speed as it heads for deeper water in the center of the lagoon.

"Nice fish", says Derrick and poles the

boat after him. "He doesn't look that big", I reply.

"I think you will be surprised", he assures.

I am thinking to myself, "This shouldn't take too long".

Derrick poles the boat after the fish. I gain line rapidly and in no time nearly all of the backing is on the reel. I actually turn the fish around, so he is facing me. I see his gray outline against the bottom.

Suddenly, there is an explosion when the Permit panics, turns end for end and the rod is nearly wrenched from my grip. The reel shrieks, its handle is a blur. Fifty yards of backing melts from the spool and then he turns the afterburner on, taking another hundred yards with such speed that I can hear the reel handle churning air like a turbine. Then he stops and just wanders around, and I realize that it was my image on the bow which had spooked him, not the tension of the line. I pull hard but it seems to have little effect. Derrick poles the boat and once again the line is gained back to the reel and the Permit spooks and takes it away. This process is repeated many times with the Permit showing unbelievable resistance. However, the runs do keep getting shorter and shorter.

Over an hour later it was getting dark when the Permit was finally tailed. My right arm is in shock from wrist to elbow. Derrick is elated. The Permit is thirty-one inches long and possibly over fifteen pounds, much larger than it had appeared in the water. I stare in awe at this beautiful silvery creature in my hands and then place it gently in the water. It revives quickly and churns out into the tropical sunset. There is much laughter in the boat as Derrick fires up the motor and we head back for camp.

The next day I was able to land a nearly identical Permit which almost spooled me. The day after that Jim got a double. The first was about twelve pounds, the other around twenty. All of the fish were taken on the brownish gray fly. We named it the Placencia Mud Crab. Now we had a fly that permit would eat. Our confidence grew. On that trip I landed two more permits. On the next, our third trip, I landed five. Our fourth trip was the best ever for me, landing fourteen out of nineteen. On that trip I was able to land five permits in one day. Patty caught Permit every trip too, but she didn't go as crazy for it as I did.

In a total of ten, ten-day trips, where permit fishing took up about 40% of the time, I landed forty-two permits. That comes to about a permit a day for 40 days. That makes Permit fishing comparable with steelhead fishing for the same ten-year period; 1983-1993. Nothing out fished the Placencia Mud Crabs in the mud bottom lagoons where over half of our permit were caught. We also encountered permit over hard bottom coral flats. In these habitats permit foods were more diverse. Flies that represented olive crabs, small minnows, shrimp, and urchins were most productive.

By the mid 1990's the Belize fishery had started to decline, and we quit fishing there for a while. In 2008 Belize passed a law to protect their saltwater fly-fishing industry. Now the only reason you can possess a bonefish, permit or tarpon is for catch and release. We fished again in Belize in 2012 and 2014 and the fishery had regained its former productivity. In 2020 Belize banned gill nets. There is no factor that leads to a happier ending than conservation minded fish management.

Chapter 25

Opening Your Eyes

"The secret of success is to do the common thing uncommonly well."

--John D. Rockefeller Jr.

Guides and clients can have a love/hate relationship especially when they are both alphas. The harder the lesson the more it sticks in your mind. The harder it sticks the more it becomes part of your soul.

Derrick Muschamp, of Placencia, Belize was certainly one of the most physically imposing individuals I have ever met. When compared against the other blacks in his community, his features were a little too sharp and angular to be pure Negro. His hair was shiny black, but wavy, not curly. His skin is golden brown, instead of chocolate brown. When asked about his lineage, he replied that his great, great, great grandfather had been a Portuguese pirate on a British privateer. At thirty-five, Derrick stood six foot one and weighed a rock solid two hundred and seventy five pounds. Because of his low fat content, he looked deceptively slim. His true size was realized only when we first shook hands. His thumbs were the size of turkey eggs. His bare calves were the size of my thighs. His wrists were the size of my ankles. When reappraised Derrick's torso was massive, like the trunk of a tree. Added to that, Derrick displayed the balance of a ballet dancer as he poled his blue and white wooden skiff while walking a five-inch wide gunnel that ran across the stern and both sides of the boat. He poled from the rear, either side or the front of the boat. Most days he would be constantly on the move as he skillfully maneuvered this heavy built Belizean boat through many narrow tidal creeks and flats channels. Where American captains use composite push poles that are measured in ounces, Derrick's hard wood pole weighed about thirty-five pounds. Because of his immense strength, he handled it effortlessly. Derrick's vision was nearly superhuman, and it was not only that he spotted fish, but also literally saw everything else around him. His ocular acuity worked nearly as good at night in the pitch black.

Derrick was a tireless hunter and a provider of high-powered fly fishing drama. His home waters were full of big powerful fish. He had learned his fishery first-hand as both a diver and fishing guide. He believed that scientific insight was an ingredient of fly fishing success, and he studied his surroundings using keen senses and recording the details with his extraordinary sharp memory. He understood the habits of tarpon and bonefish as well as most of the other reef dwellers, but most enjoyed hunting for Permit. In that he was a hundred lifetimes more advanced than the next best Permit guide I ever fished with. Derrick not only knew where to find Permit, but also how to catch them. When you were hunting Permit with Derrick, he might make you feel like you were the focus of the hunt, but deep inside you realized that you were simply along for the ride.

Derrick was usually charming and soft spoken, especially around the ladies. He was always fair and even-up with me on everything we did together. He figured out in a hurry that my sole purpose for hiring him was to learn everything he knew about his fish and fishery. He willingly served as my mentor but could be ruthlessly candid if my lack of awareness were slowing the process down.

This day found us alone in a shallow mud bottomed tidal lagoon of about four hundred acres. A cruel wind blew from the north, across the mangrove-covered coast of southern Belize and into our faces. It whipped the surface of the lagoon into foot high chop. The waves were violent enough to stir up the silty bottom in the water that averaged eighteen inches deep. This turned the normally clear lagoon to something near the consistency of chocolate milk. For me, the visibility in the water had dropped to zero. My companion didn't seem to be impeded in the least.

He called out from the back of his boat, "Permit, ten o'clock, fifty feet, coming at you slowly."

Try as I might, I could not see it. Suddenly there was a boil of muddy water and a vee- wake as the fish spooked from where Derrick had said. It was a chance not capitalized upon. My heart sunk at the missed opportunity.

The boat continued against the wind for another twenty minutes. Derrick called again, "Permit one o-clock, thirty feet, facing to the right."

Derrick held the boat against the wind with his push pole. And tried to direct me. I never saw the fish until it bolted. Another easy shot was blown. Derrick's voice remained calm. Inside I was seething with disappointment. During the prior five days of this same trip, I landed three permit and it had only whetted my appetite.

Again, Derrick called out the direction and distance on a fish I was unable to see in time to deliver a cast. It too ran off with a plume of mud and a violent vee-wake.

Derrick commented that I was not following his directions and reiterated that twelve o'clock was the centerline of the boat.

After a fourth fish was blown, I reeled in my line, and turning on the front deck to face him, I pleaded, "Derrick, I can't see the fish. How do you see fish in this kind of water?"

Derrick looked me straight in the eye and said with conviction, "It's easy mon, just open your fucking eyes and you will see them!"

"I beg your pardon," was my indignant reply? "We have discussed this issue before. You're not paying attention! Open your fucking

eyes. You Americans view everything like you are looking down a pipe. God gave you peripheral vision, but you're too fucking lazy to use it!"

Men don't usually talk to me in that tone of voice. I try to make sure no one ever gets away with it. It's the completely confident tone like an enraged father talking to a wayward son, like an adult talking to a child. Rage welled up inside me. Suddenly I wanted to tear Derrick off the back of the boat and hold his head under water. There was only one little problem; Derrick had a hundred pounds of dynamite on me. There was no possibility I could get the job done. I had to suck it up.

Derrick spread his hands on wide swept arms. Do this, he instructed." You can still see your hands.

Then he held one hand at his crotch level and the other far above his eyes. You can still see your hands. Practice using your peripheral vision. You spot permit with your peripheral vision. Do it!"

Still seething, I turned my back on him. Dispelling wishes for a large weapon, it finally sunk into my thick skull that he had just gambled on our friendship for something he thought was important. And yes, we had discussed the "how to see fish" subject several times before.

I stood on the bow of the boat with my eyes wide open, trying to see directly in front of me to the horizon and as far to each side as possible. There was so much unaccustomed information streaming into my visual cortex that I felt stoned. For a while even my balance became impaired, and just standing upright on the casting platform was a challenge. After about twenty minutes my mind began to clear, and the world began to stabilize.

The world looks different when you use all your vision. There are no apparent hard edges at the extremity, yet everything can be very clear and well defined. I became fascinated with this new worldview and found that I not only became comfortable with it, but also enthralled with the exploration of it.

Suddenly in the extreme periphery of my left

eye appeared the dorsal fin, tail, and black back of a medium size Permit. At that point everything in the world slowed down and became extremely clear. My back cast was already in the air when Derrick called from behind me, “Permit nine o’clock, forty feet…coming at you. The speed and angle of the cast were computed to the cruising speed, angle, and depth of the fish. The cast was delivered with relaxed muscles and confident psyche. The heavy crab fly tugged gently letting me know that the leader was completely straight behind me. The rod loaded only in the tip with smooth acceleration. The stop at the end of the stroke was perfectly timed. The loop formed and unfolded with delicacy and speed. The heavy crab fly plopped gently to the water, four feet ahead of and directly in the path of the oncoming fish. The fly sunk on a perfectly tight line. When the fish was within two feet of the fly, I pulled on the line with my left hand…tug, tug…to make the fly look like a crab that was trying to dig himself down into the silty bottom. The fish nosed down. The line tightened a little more from the weight of the fish. I made a one- foot strip. The line came up tight and the water exploded as the hook penetrated the fleshy mouth. The first run was over a hundred fifty yards into the backing. Then it took another fifty yards in two short bursts. Fortunately, the Permit had run for the open water at the center of the lagoon, and not back into the mangroves. The fight was long and hard against the stiff ten- weight rod and sixteen pound-test tippets. Derrick tailed the fish after nearly an hour, and I was surprised to see that it only weighed about twelve pounds. But I was elated. I had spotted that Permit before the guide had called its position. That meant I was becoming an equal member of the team. Derrick, who always likes to celebrate the landing of a permit, was elated and very friendly. My attitude toward him warmed slightly, but in the back of my mind there was the extreme discomfort of being talked down-to, and the edges of my mind were still asking for retribution. I let that thought fade at the realization of my recent accomplishment and the lesson that had arrived with it. I could spot Permit with Derrick's peripheral vision technique. I had to adapt it into my everyday eyesight. The Permit was released, and we continued after another.

Derrick and I were silent as we worked our way around the lagoon. The wind had abated, and the surface of the water had smoothed out. A wet stripe on the trunks of the mangroves revealed that the tide was dropping. Maybe the water in the lagoon was becoming too shallow and the Permits were leaving. I began to doubt if we would see another one. The bottom of my feet began to ache from standing on the hard deck for so long. Yet, I consciously practiced seeing with my peripheral vision. Another hour went by and the water in the lagoon became even shallower. I was about to say to Derrick that we ought to take a break when there was a glint of something out of the corner of my left eye. It was the tip of a Permit dorsal fin reflecting the afternoon sun. It disappeared and then reappeared twenty feet farther to the right. I shifted my stance and looked over my right shoulder to see if Derrick were in the way of my back-cast. He wasn't. He was poling from the left corner of the boat. The Permit was seventy- five feet from the boat. I shot line on the back cast and a bunch more on the forward cast. The fly landed six feet directly ahead of the fish. As the fish approached the fly, I twitched it. The Permit accelerated and sucked up the fly going away from me. I held onto the line and the fish hooked himself.

This fish was larger and stronger than the previous one. It took over an hour to land the eighteen-pounder. To date that was the largest permit I had caught.

I was nearly ready to congratulate myself on seeing a Permit the guide had missed, when Derrick complemented me on my newly acquired skill and noted that he had seen me find the fish when only the tip of the dorsal fin was above the surface. Who knows how long he had been watching the fish before I had seen it? It appeared that the apprentice would need more time to become a master, but at least the process had finally begun.

Chapter 26

The Road in Belize

Ooh, the wheel in the sky keeps on turnin'

--Journey

Patty and I had been on a fly-fishing vacation for ten days and had seen offshore keys and much of Belize's shoreline from a boat, but we had yet to visit the interior we had seen from the air when we flew south from Belize City to Placencia, a small village in the Stann Creek district of Belize.

I asked Dalton, the owner of the Paradise Hotel, our temporary base camp, if he could hire us a driver with a car to show us the surrounding countryside. Next morning, we were met at our room by Alejandro, a tall slim black man who appeared to be in his twenties. He had a solid-looking ten-year-old Ford pickup. We laid out a basic itinerary, agreed on a price and were soon on our way.

In 1983, the Hummingbird Highway was still a dusty two-lane gravel road running south from Belmopan, bypassing Dangriga, Hopkins, and Placencia and ending at Punta Gorda in the Toledo District in the southernmost part of Belize. It was the newest stretch of a highway that connected the entire country. Belize had been British Honduras, a Crown Colony established in 1871. Then in 1981 it achieved full independence and a new name but remained a member of the British Commonwealth of Nations, and a British Military Protectorate. When bordering Guatemala claimed sovereignty over Belize, Britain sent the Queens Guard with Naval escorts and Harrier jets to enforce its policy of total non-interference. The Hummingbird Highway was built as a strategic asset to quickly move troops and equipment.

During our journey, parts of the roadbed and some bridges remained under construction. Rather than pass straight across the country it meandered through small population centers, its grade far enough from the foot of the Maya Mountains to avoid their geological chaos and the expense of building a road through mountainous terrain. Traversing a gently sloping coastal plain it transitioned into rolling hills and randomly spaced meandering river valleys flowing from the mountains to the Caribbean.

After a pleasant but uneventful ten-mile journey south, Alejandro explained that a bridge we were approaching was new. All the river-crossing bridges had been built during the last two summers by the British military. Before then the only roads were intermittent ruts through the jungle. He believed in two years the road would be paved, shortening the drive to Belize City to a day.

Beneath the bridge ran a sizeable aqua-colored spring creek where a dozen black-haired, brown-bodied naked women were washing clothes.

We stopped a quarter mile beyond the bridge at a Maya Indian village comprised of palapa-roofed, bamboo-walled, dirt-floored huts lacking closing doors or windows to hide their meager contents. In the center of the village, a new building was under construction on stilts, its floor eight feet above ground. Perched Atop its deck it looked like the rest in the village. Rough-sawed decking extended on all sides several feet beyond its walls. Above deck, the house was mostly finished except for a space at the peak of its thatched roof.

At first, the village seemed empty. Then a few people appeared at its far end, a group aged from children to elderly, small in stature and lightly built. They looked vibrant and healthy, with white teeth and broad smiles. A small middle-aged barefooted man with blue jeans, light- blue long-sleeved shirt, and a frayed straw hat approached us and introduced himself in fluent English as “Juan.” Juan wanted to know where we were from, how long we had been in Belize, how many Maya communities we had visited, how we liked Belize, and how long we were staying.

"We're from Oregon, near Mount Hood. It's a huge snow-capped volcano, east of Portland," I replied. "This is our first visit to Belize. We like it fine so far. This is our first Mayan village and our first-ever vacation."

Juan's smile widened. He was joined by a slim middle-aged woman wearing a shawl and carrying a shallow cardboard tray containing strips of cloth. Juan explained that his wife Mahin did embroidery for sale and asked if we'd like to buy some. I introduced Mahin to Patty, and Juan and I left them to get acquainted while we continued our tour of the village.

Conversing quietly and laughing, more people appeared from every direction, filling the clean orderly landscape of well-kept palapa homes backgrounded by lush green jungle foliage. I was struck by their happiness and mentioned this to Juan.

"The art of nothingness works for them," he said.

"What do you mean," I asked. "The art of nothingness?"

"When the Spanish came five-hundred years ago, we were a proud, flamboyant people with grand buildings and fancy clothes. We thought we could control our destinies. But the Spanish had horses and guns. Their armies were stronger, and with them came diseases that weakened us. They slaughtered our armies, stole our women and possessions, and made slaves of us. The only way we could remain free was to disappear into the jungle, and if found appear humble with nothing of value. We avoided capture with little more than the clothes on our backs, hiding in empty dirt-floor huts in the jungle to avoid capture.

We lived like this for a dozen generations until the English came and drove the Spaniards away. The English ignored us unless we interfered with their timber harvest. When the big trees were gone, they had no more use for the jungle. We were completely alone, as we had been thousands of years ago. Now we know that power and possessions do not bring happiness. Our lives are simpler, free of hoarded possessions. Now the forest and rivers provide everything we need. But a new road has been built, and our world is changing again."

Patty and I had come here on that road as tourists, student travelers amazed by a reality we never thought existed. When Patty rejoined us, she showed me a strip of intricately embroidered cloth she had purchased and put it in her backpack. Juan asked if we would like to see how his people raised corn. A couple of hundred yards on a narrow trail brought us to a garden in the jungle. We smelled charcoal before light from an open canopy revealed a clearing and a prime example of primitive slash and burn agriculture. In this village, at twelve degrees off the equator corn grew year-round, three generations at a time, planted in perfectly parallel rows fifty yards long and five feet apart. At one end of the garden were twelve rows of corn plants six inches apart, three to four inches tall. In the middle of the garden were twelve rows of corn, same distance apart, three feet tall. At the other end were twelve rows, same length, same distance, but eight feet tall with maturing ears from six inches to over a foot long, the largest ready for harvest. Nowhere were there any weeds showing. Throughout the garden charred tree trunks were left where they had fallen during the fire. No limbs, brush, or stumps remained, only trunks larger than six inches in diameter. It took less than an acre of garden to provide enough corn to feed the entire village year-round.

Having grown up on a farm, I had spent many hours planting, hoeing, weeding, and harvesting vegetables. My parents were farming perfectionists, but nowhere had I seen it better than this. I asked Juan why they had left the burnt logs. They seemed to be in the way. “Nutrients,” he replied. “Corn likes charcoal.”

A few minutes later we were back in the village. I told Juan that part of my background was in building houses, and I was curious about how other cultures built theirs. I asked him about the house on stilts. He said the Mayas had built houses the same for thousands of years, but after the road came it was easier for them to travel. They had noticed the houses of the black people had some advantages. Wooden-floored houses were easier to keep clean. Houses on stilts had better air circulation, their floors were drier and more comfortable and secure. This was the first house on stilts in Juan's village. But it was also more expensive. Lumber had to be sawn at a mill and the floor nailed. To make it last, the floor must be painted every three years.

I asked Juan who owned the new house, thinking it would be the mayor or headman. His answer surprised me. It was for a young couple who were to be married in a couple of weeks. In this and surrounding villages, God chose marriage partners and families made the arrangements. Marriage partners had no say in the matter.

"When a boy child is born, the next unrelated girl child is to become his wife," Juan said. "They came into the world near to the same time to live together. When they reach puberty, their families build them a house. After they marry, they move into their new home."

We climbed into Alejandro's pickup for a ride farther down the Hummingbird Highway to our next destination. As we drove, I thought how different that Maya village is from where I live in Oregon. I remembered reading in Carlos Castaneda's cult classics of the 1960s about how Yaqui Indian shamans believed that a man's possessions do nothing but rob him of power.

Ten miles from the village we stopped at a small pullout with a wooden sign, Nim La Punit Archeological Site 1 Mile. No other cars were parked along the road. Nim La Punit means "Big is the Hat" in Kekchi Maya for a repugnant-looking character with a large headdress deeply incised into the largest of twenty-six sandstone stelae discovered at the ruin in 1976. The site might have been inhabited as late as 800 A.D., during the time of the first Viking raids in England and at the peak of the classic Maya period.

Hiking up a steep trail near the sign, we had climbed about two hundred yards when it started to rain. For twenty minutes the three of us sheltered under a single six-foot diameter leaf while water poured off on all sides around us. The storm passed quickly, and we entered the freshly bathed ancient city in fragrant, warm sunlight. Stelae were strewn all over the ground with only a few upright in their original positions, kiosks of the Maya world, educational signs displaying past events, or the life histories of important people. The exposed walls were assembled from flagstones stacked without mortar. We spent less than an hour there and hiked back to the pickup.

Another five-mile drive and another hike brought us to Lubaantun, "Place of the Fallen Stones," a much larger site than Nim La Punit, this one complete with a working archaeologist in residence who introduced himself as Diego. Much land had been cleared, exposing numerous structures in various stages of dilapidation. Their architectural plan had followed the natural features of a long semicircular ridge about two hundred feet above the ocean, the ridge's spine fashioned into a ceremonial center complete with plazas, three ball courts, and various temples. The seaside of the ridge had apparently been agriculturally terraced to the narrow flat coastal plain below.

The near side of the ridge had not been cleared of jungle, so it was hard to determine the true nature of cultivation.

Diego pointed to a spot where two small rivers emptied into a shining bay below us and said there was evidence it had once been a seaport. As he walked us through the site, explaining the significance of their different structures, he pointed to a tall pyramid-shaped ruin with a large conical depression on its top and told us that some of the first so-called archeologists had been nothing but looters: "In 1924, a guy named Fredrich Michael Hedges dynamited the top off that building looking for a tomb with treasure."

Fredrich Michael Hedges could have been a real-life model for Hollywood's Indiana Jones. Hedges traveled with a beautiful noblewoman, Lady Richmond Brown, his partner, and financier during Hedges' adventures at Lubaantun. By her own account, Anna Michael Hedges, his adopted daughter, claimed to have also been on this expedition and discovered a life-sized clear crystal skull reputed to have many powers. This "magical Skull of Doom" was allegedly found at the bottom of the depression excavated by the dynamite blast. Fredrich Michael Hedges and the dynamite blast were real, but Anna Hedges and her Crystal Skull of Doom are regarded with great suspicion by most scholars of ancient artifacts. The skull's manufacturer remains unproven.

Lubaantun is unusual for a Mayan site. No mortar or limestone was used in its construction. The squared building stones of black slate were stacked with "in-and-out" designs. Many of the buildings had radiused, round corners. I sat on ancient steps contemplating a stone wall made of thousands of symmetrical squared stones and wondered how it could have been built without metal tools, wheels, or draft animals. A single stone caught my attention. It had fallen from the wall and was squared with sharp, parallel edges and dimensions identical to the thousands like it. How had the Mayans been able to shape even a single stone so perfectly? I still can't understand the precision that existed during the stone age. I thought of Juan's corn patch with its perfect parallel rows growing through blackened, jack- strawed tree trunks. It was time, patience and relentless trial and error. It was Mayan engineering before engines. It was an inventive genius.

According to Diego, the Mayas who lived in Lubaantun had harvested the Belize Reef much like today's residents. Archaeological excavations have revealed numerous fish bones and conch shells. Through most sedimentary layers the conch shells were from full-sized adults about a foot in length, but just before the Mayans abandoned their site, they had eaten baby conchs with shells mostly three to four inches in length. The Mayan's population had grown and exceeded the reef's capacity to sustain them. Most Mayan cities collapsed during this same period. In twenty years, the Yucatan's population shrank from over twelve million to two hundred thousand. A regional drought was thought to be the cause. The rain stopped, agriculture failed, and the people starved to death…eventually the rain restarted…the jungle regrew…the few people lived in the jungle…then someone built a road…

Chapter 27

Hatchery Trees

"Nature does not hurry, yet everything is accomplished."

--Loa Tzu

View the clear desert sky at 3:00 a.m. from the bottom of the Deschutes River Canyon to get a non-biased perspective on your life. Almost everything above the canyon rim is filled with the Milky Way, our massive ancient home galaxy, containing an estimated 200 billion stars. The night sky appears to be static, frozen in time, as does your hard, stable footing. You could believe that you are alone in a wilderness, transported to a simpler place and time where complete understanding is easy. That you're shielded from the civilized world's reckless pace that blurs reality, forcing you to keep up with technology and the deceptions created by the rest of humanity. Here in the canyon, you can observe the water flow and watch trees grow. You study how things work in this place because everything here is real and moving so slow it is easy to understand.

As you shall see, nothing could be further from the truth. Earth is moving 66,616 mph while continuously orbiting the sun. Our whole solar system is traveling approximately 514,495 mph in its 230-million-year orbit around the center of the Milky Way Galaxy, traveling at 1.3 million miles per hour to who knows where. Everything is changing continually, and understanding any of it may be an illusion, but we try.

When I started fishing the Deschutes in the mid-1960s, the landscape was controlled by large ranches whose livestock dominated the canyon. They concentrated next to the water where the vegetation was. Most of the backdrop was barren dirt, bedrock, and scrabble. The ground cover had all but disappeared since Peter Skein Ogdon had described "a sea of grass higher than a horse's belly" from his expedition through the region in 1830. That report had attracted the attention of cattlemen like Pete French, who brought thousands of domestic cattle to feast on the bounty. Thousands more sheep followed the cattle. When they got done, the grass had been pulled up by the roots. The land was ruined. The native grass was nearly extinct, replaced by spindly Eurasian species such as cheatgrass throughout Oregon east of the Cascades, including the Deschutes River Canyon.

In the 1970s, a young lawyer by the name of Doug Robertson started fishing with one of the first jet boat guides, Jerry Todd. Todd had a camp across the river from the mouth of Harris Canyon. One night while sitting around the campfire, Doug asked Jerry who owned the land they were camping on. Jerry replied he didn't know. Doug did a land search and found the parcel belonged to a corporation registered in San Francisco called The Oregon Covered Wagon Road Company, which wanted to divest themselves of it. Doug immediately started putting together a business plan to buy the stocks in the company to monopolize access to the Lower Deschutes River and turn it into a sportsmen's paradise for a few rich guys. In the end, the idea turned out to be socially and financially unfeasible. At that point, Doug had a change of heart and instead set up a nonprofit called the Oregon Wildlife Heritage Foundation to raise money, acquire the land, and turn it over to the Oregon State Parks Department. This program proved so popular in the early 1980s that the funds exceeded the initial goals. Eventually, public access was acquired, and livestock was excluded from the bottom of the canyon for the lower fifty miles.

Once the livestock was removed from the riparian zone, the land started a process of revegetation. At first, only low plants and grass grew next to the water's edge. Then little alder trees and other brush also sprouted. I was fascinated with an observation of the process. The green strip got wider every season as the capillary action caused by the vegetation moved water further and further from the river's edge. The growth of the alder trees was incredibly explosive, becoming far more successful than I could have ever imagined possible.

My fishing camp is perched on a high bank above the river. It gives us a great view of the river from under a canopy of giant sumacs. A day between customers has left me alone.

A frigid gusting downstream breeze had killed my enthusiasm for fishing. Instead, I had elected to fire up the nearly silent Honda generator and catalytic heater to work inside our fully enclosed dining tent with my laptop computer.

Voices came from across the river muffled by the tent's thin sidewall curtains, which moved with every pulse of the cold October wind. My subconscious had sorted out two different pitches of sounds that tracked the two male anglers as they progressed the length of great steelhead water on the far shore. It had lasted an hour. It was time to leave the warmth of the tent and offer hospitality to these unseen and still unknown anglers before they left the area. My tent provided a respite from the wind, but I needed a break from my keyboard, and thought some company might be entertaining.

A dark green raft was tied to an alder across the

river. Two anglers armed with Spey tackle were returning to the boat. One had walked far upstream, and the other had started at the boat but was returning from far downstream. They were the voices I had been listening to. I recognized the boat and both men; they were Tom and Bill. This pair has a reputation as some of the region's most resolute and hardworking wild fish conservation advocates. I kept an eye on them while going through my routine, and when they were done fishing and readying the boat to leave, I yelled across the river that there was a fresh pot of coffee and a full bottle of Bailey's Irish Cream if they wanted to row over. Both enthusiastically accepted my invitation. My friends were ushered inside the tent, and they vigorously took steaming cups of fresh coffee liberally laced with liqueur.

After the usual exchange of fishing reports, the discussion of fishery management seemed unavoidable. These two guys have an intense dislike for fish hatcheries, claiming that hatchery fish spawning with wild fish dilutes the genetic viability of wild stocks.

I tried to turn the conversation to a more positive subject by saying, "Boy, those alders are sure coming back after the livestock were removed."

Bill replied, "Ya, we planted those trees."

It took me totally by surprise, "You planted alder trees? I thought you wanted everything wild?"

"Yes, we came in here in two offseasons and planted 30,000 alder trees."

My mind recoiled as it realized that everything, I thought was nature healing itself from abuse of people and their animals was a lie. My indignation boiled through the surface, "How did you get a permit to do that?"

Bill answered with an air of self-righteousness, "We didn't; we just did it! Who's going to object to us planting trees?"

"Bill, are those wild trees, or are they hatchery trees?"

Suddenly, he was defensive, "Those are wild trees from the Alder Conservancy over on the John Day River!"

"So, you brought trees from a different watershed and planted them here. What is the difference between hatchery trees and hatchery steelhead?"

Two well-intentioned but unhappy men left camp - our bond broken. The question never got answered. In 2018, the giant Substation Range Fire burnt and killed nearly every tree in the canyon, both wild and hatchery. Ironically, wildness had the last say in its purest form: fire. It will take years for trees to grow back, but they will. No one seems to care if they are all wild or not.

In my estimation, the Substation Range Fire was a cataclysm, but it did provide an immediate advantage. It burnt all the evergreen blackberry patches to the bare dirt, making impenetrable growth areas accessible. At a BLM Guide meeting, I pointed out that this invasive species was libel to take over and block human traffic on the canyon floor. With the advent of the fire, we had a unique opportunity to take control of the situation. BLM was unresponsive, and the chance was lost.

As you gaze from the bottom of the canyon at 3:00 in the morning, you might console yourself with, "Does any of this matter?" Do stickery invasive blackberries block human traffic? No doubt about it. Is that good or bad, might be the next question? Do hatchery trees versus wild trees matter to the Milky Way Galaxy and its 200 billion stars, or any of its billions of planets, or the billions of galaxies with stars and planets, or the Universe with its unquantifiable scale? Should it have to provide the answer? Who should be responsible? Anyone? Does anyone have the right to ask the question? Has anyone asked it before? If so, was there an answer?

Chapter 28

The Effects of Beavers

"Man is the most insane of species. He worships an invisible God
and destroys a visible Nature. Unaware that this Nature he's destroying
is this God he's worshiping."

--Hubert Reeves

The rag-tag farm boy in beat-up Converse High Tops knew there would be a new beaver dam crossing the creek before he could see it. He could hear the tinkling of the water falling through the downstream edge of the dam and noted the opening on the timbered island where the animals had been falling aspens. Chips littered the hard, packed earth around the base of tree stumps where the animals had stood on their huge, webbed hind feet and balanced on their strong flat tails as they chewed the trees in two, falling them toward the creek with precision.

There were neat trails of drag marks to the water where the beavers had transported the dismembered limbs and trunks of the trees and sunk their woody treasure into the deepened water. It was a temporary dam that would not survive next spring's runoff, maybe not even the rising waters of winter rains. The boy approached the dam cautiously, for he knew what he would find there. He crouched and waited, watching the flow below the dam through the screen of sticks protruding from the lower edge of the spillway. He was relaxed and sure.

Then, there it was: a tiny splash different from the cadence of free flowing water. A large fish was holding below the dam and the boy saw it move then marked the placement. He slipped silently into the water of the pond held by the dam until he lay belly down over the dam submerged up to his armpits and slowly moved his right arm down through the layer of sticks overhanging the moving water. He could see the fish clearly but stretched his reach further until he could feel the slick back of the fish and very gently petted it. The fish felt the gentle touch and backed slowly downriver with its gills flaring until the notch where the gill plate joined the head encountered the boy's middle finger. The movement was swift and deadly as the finger came through the gill opening on one side and was met by the opposing thumb coming through the open gill plate from the other side. The big bull trout writhed but the grip was hardened by years of milking cows and the fish was helpless in the grip of the strong hand. The success of this human predator was made possible by the stream passage obstruction set in place by the stout, aquatic rodents, North American Beavers. The boy was born during WWII but was practicing skills attained by humans long before they acquired fire, clothing, weapons, or tools. To catch large fish like the primitive boy the only tool needed was an opposing thumb. Weapons might have been first developed to protect hand fishing places from competition with bears and other critters who thought cold water fish tasted good. You might want to speculate on an age of man with an opposing thumb before fire, where fish were grabbed and ate raw. I'm betting that humans, large salmonids, and beavers have shared the same parts of the planet for a very long time, and in no time in perfect harmony… and at no time any more disharmonious for them than this time. It seems possible that fish and humans have shared habitat with beavers in Europe for about six hundred thousand years. My hope is that we can coexist for six hundred thousand more. I was born into the end of an age when young men prowled chilled forests with implements fashioned to harvest protein. I remember the smells of frost turning into mist rising from all the surfaces of a North Idaho yellowed aspen forest and an October beaver pond full of bright colored brookies.

Beavers have the unique ability to thrive by

eating the cambium layer of bark of certain species of deciduous trees such as willows, poplars, and cottonwoods, all of which flourish in wetlands. Beavers may be the first mammalian agriculturists, creating habitats specifically modified to suit their favorite trees and plants. Modern beavers live for an average of ten years and weigh 35 to 50 pounds, but some rare individuals can exceed one hundred pounds. North American Beavers, *Castor canadensis,* showed up in the fossil record about a million years ago, but the beaver family tree goes back much further - try 35 to 45-million years! During the millions of years that followed, about thirty genera of beavers have evolved then vanished. The oldest evidence of a beaver pond is from a dig on Ellesmere Island in the Canadian far north. Paleontologist, Natalia Rybczynski, excavated Ellesmere Pond and found remains of a dam built twenty-four million years ago by extinct predecessors to modern beavers. Beavers are perfectly adapted to the lifestyle they have chosen. To facilitate the harvesting of food they have an upper and lower set of chisel-shaped self-sharpening teeth. The coating at the very front of each tooth is very hard and the rest of the tooth is softer. Each tooth is rooted deep in the skull and lower jaw for maximum strength. The teeth grow continuously, so beavers must use their teeth regularly to keep them at the right length. It's possible for a single beaver to fall trees more than two feet in diameter in a single night, though most trees harvested by beavers are less than half that size.

Many beavers live in rivers that are too large to dam and must burrow into a bank for security. In rivers such as the Clackamas and Sandy Rivers, in Northwestern Oregon, there are channels eroded out of mudstone, an ancient seafloor sedimentary deposit. Mudstone is soft enough that with a little work you could scratch your name into it with a large nail, but hard enough that you will have to go over the lettering several times to be able to read it. Yet, beavers can excavate a tunnel with their teeth starting below the low water mark before continuing several feet into the bank, then rising a couple of feet above the high water mark. In these fluctuating rivers, the elevation increase in the tunnel might be three to eight feet before creating a four-foot diameter living chamber with a ceiling height of three to four feet. Though it is a lot of riverbanks being transported and discarded, beavers that live this lifestyle don't change the topography or influence fish habitat very much. Many pools in these rivers are deep enough to protect the animals and their food cache.

Beavers who utilize smaller, lower gradient streams change their habitat to a greater extent. To start a colony, a pair of beavers will find a small stream with the right complement of resources, then work to build a dam that forms a pond. Beavers use the natural terrain to locate a choke point where they can most easily build a dam. They then fill the dam site with logs and sticks woven together with rocks, mud, leaves, and grass to form a barrier that raises the water level just enough to enable them to easily fall timber into the pond as it is forming. This allows them to make a secure underwater cache of tree parts for food and construction materials. In time, this cache might become a warehouse of food for use during the winter months. Beavers are master construction engineers and efficiency experts. Examination of dams shows the highest percentage of wooden parts were trimmed to the right length and stripped of bark; the cambium layer eaten before the wooden piece was placed in the dam. Beavers might have invented the multiple-use strategy.

As they harvest all the timber easily reached from the level of their pond, they raise the water level by adding to the size of their dam, inundating more land, and accessing more timber for their cache. As the beaver family grows, it expands territory. The younger pairs of beavers move up- or downstream, where the process begins again. After several generations, instead of one or two ponds the extended beaver family manages several dozen ponds that form a great complex. The only limitations are the amount of water and the topography that holds it; however, beavers always engineer for maximum results.

Eventually, bedload shift in the stream will fill some ponds with silt and turn the stream canyon into a meadow, creating the perfect habitat for all the kinds of foods that beavers like to eat. After a hundred generations of dam-building beavers, the whole lower story of the canyon becomes a vast meadow complex of beaver ponds. This may include thousands of acres of rich silty soil with a high water table, a vast earthen sponge. Cool water moves slowly through these low gradient beaver-made habitats absorbing soluble nutrients in the process. It's because of this process that dams built by beavers expand wild fish habitats, something that humans building industrial age dams don't always achieve.

In his authoritative work: *Eager: The Surprising Secret Life of Beavers and Why They Matter*, Ben Goldfarb studied beavers with experts across the United States and Europe. Beaver ponds leave a long-lasting footprint on the landscape. Since old and current beaver dam complexes are easily identified from space, a study was conducted analyzing topographic satellite photos of North

America. This project revealed the probable surface area of beaver ponds in what became The United States, before the influx of Europeans, was roughly equal to the land now held inside the borders of Nevada and Arizona combined. When beaver populations were at their peak, water flow in every watershed they inhabited moved more slowly and water levels and temperatures were more stable. In places where beaver populations declined, the water flow rate turned from months to weeks or even hours. This had a drastic influence on dissolved nutrients and the chemical composition of the water itself. The longer you soak a tea bag, the darker the tea. The water in most beaver dam complexes is tea-colored, rich in dissolved plant matter.

Somehow, trout and salmon are always able to find their way through these labyrinths of beaver dams and prefer them as rearing habitat for anadromous fish and living habitat for resident fish. With the beaver colony in place, instead of a steep little stream with room enough for a couple of pairs of salmon, there might be enough habitat to spawn, rear, and return a hundred pairs of salmon. Within ancient beaver pond meadow complexes that had been used through the last ice age, you might have a stream with thousands of salmon spawning and dying.

In such a meadow, every salmon carcass is a

packet of nutrients brought from the ocean to be shared by all of the inhabitants living where they spawn and die. The water becomes so rich and so predictable with its flows that it has the capacity of many modern hatcheries. Perhaps the cliché of "the salmon were so thick we could have walked across the river on them" wasn't just boastful imagery but true.

Beavers have unique fur that allows them to cope with the wet cold environment they thrived in. A square inch of a hide is covered by an average of 126,000 individual hairs, more than an individual human has on its head. The hair is in two specialized layers: the outer layer is composed of shiny, two-inch long, stiff, tapered, solid, resilient guard hairs and the protected inner layer of shorter, finer fur, which is waterproof insulation that keeps these aquatic rodents warm. Unfortunately for this race of animals, their fur was found to retain its water resistance even when turned into felt hats. For this process, all the guard hairs are plucked and only the fine fur was used for felt. The resulting practical good looks resulted in a men's fashion craze that created demand and an economic boom that lasted for several hundred years. Beaver felt hats are still in Vogue today. If you don't believe it, check the prices of top of the line Stetson or Resistol American western style headwear.

Apparently beavers and native North Americans had lived in balance for thousands of years. Beavers may not have been easy prey for stone age people. When the Europeans came, they brought with them the spring steel trap. From the time Europeans came to North America, it only took them about three hundred years to trap beavers to near extinction. Quick profit was the main driving force, but international politics in the form of imperial expansion also played a part. From 1824 to 1830 Peter Skene Ogden, working as an officer of the Hudson Bay Company (English), led five trapping expeditions to eradicate beavers to extinction and turn parts of the Pacific Northwest into a fur desert to discourage American influence and migration into the region.

Within a few years, there were not enough beavers to maintain all the dams, and some began to disintegrate. As successive waves of trappers descended upon the meadows, the dams which were all made from biodegradable parts crumpled and fell to pieces. The streams sped up more with every spring flood and dug deep, narrow channels. The over-harvesting of beavers and the wholesale destruction of habitat they created was the first step in the reduction of anadromous fish in North America.

A family of pioneers built a cabin and a barn

on one side of our meadow and called it their own. With a lot of hard work, they cleared the land and raised a family. Soon the beavers were gone - there was nothing left for them to eat. Now there is a dry arroyo paralleling the paved highway where an intermittent stream produces flash floods that have cut through the spongy beaver meadow clear to the bedrock.

A lonely, forlorn, ill-maintained set of farm buildings is abandoned on the far side of the dead meadow. The work of thousands of generations of beavers is blowing away as dust in the wind, carrying with it the essence of as many generations of salmon. The ecosystem that had taken beavers twenty-five millennia to build had taken descendants of European people less than three centuries to destroy. Then after the human development of the last fifty years, little evidence of the beaver meadow remained for the current society. In most cases this was not planned but was intentional.

I had finished reading *Eager: The Surprising Secret Life of Beavers and Why They Matter*, just before a late fall steelhead trip to Hells Canyon in 2019. My wife drove and I studied the landscapes looking for evidence of beaver pond complexes turned into farmland. The examples were in a nearly endless supply. I really had the blues by the time we reached the Snake River, realizing that the era of my world perception had indeed already passed before I was even born. It had gone without even a nod from the self-proclaimed salmon conservation experts who wonder why fish runs seem ever in decline. Maybe we are altering the planet quicker than they can adapt to it. Once there was more of them. Now there are more of us. Treat the Earth not as a gift from your ancestors, but as a loan from your children.

Chapter 29

A ROLE FOR CHINOOKS

It isn't where you came from. It's where you are going that counts.

--Ella Fitzgerald

There are many indications that in the past, the Columbia River Basin in Oregon, Washington, Idaho, and British Columbia hosted much larger runs of Chinook salmon than it does today. Of the five species of Pacific Salmon, Chinooks are the best equipped to exploit highly fluctual, glacial/volcanic watersheds such as the Columbia, the steepest watershed of it's size in the world, and the largest watershed feeding directly into the Pacific Ocean.

My home water, the Sandy River, flows from the slopes of Mt. Hood into the Columbia River. It is flanked by the Clackamas river to the southwest and the Hood River to the northeast and the Deschutes River east and southeast. Each of these tributary basins are microcosms of the parent watershed. Together they form my playground and research center.

Chinook salmon populations are pivotal to the

overall fishery management scheme in this combined river system. Historically fresh from the ocean bright Chinook Salmon were present within the basin nearly year around. Some strains of Chinooks were localized near the mouth of the Columbia River, but others ranged over a thousand miles inland.

In my playground rivers spanning both sides of the Cascade Mountain Range, Chinooks were in fishable numbers year around. They comprised several different races to exploit the four seasons.

Currently all Chinook runs within the Columbia River basin are in disrepair. Only two races, spring and fall Chinooks inhabit the four tributary watersheds within my study area. Spring Chinooks are the largest spawning biomass in the upper basins and Fall Chinook are the largest spawning biomass in the lower mainstems. It appears that Spring Chinooks are being replaced by Cohos as the largest upper basin biomass in the Clackamas River. All Pacific Salmon are important contributors to the food chain in all river basins they inhabit.

Both directly and indirectly, Chinook spawn (eggs) and carcasses provide nutrients to the system. Chinook eggs are ravenously consumed by all sizes of salmonids, cotids and minnows. Salmon carcasses provide nutrients for animals, birds, insects, plants, and other fish, including their own salmon fry. All salmon runs are conveyers of nutrients flowing upstream from the ocean to the headwaters of northern tributary rivers.

Chinook fry are some of the earliest to emerge from the gravel (March-April). This emergence provides an early spring meal for trout and steelhead juveniles, which are two or more years older. Chinook fry are consumed by all fish that are large enough to eat them.

John Peterson, a fishery tech for the Mt. Hood National Forest, oversaw the Still Creek (Sandy River tributary) fish trap placed to capture downstream migrating fish. Most of the fish caught in this trap were juvenile salmon, trout, and steelhead. A small sample of each specie was killed for scientific study autopsies. According to John, the spring out-migrating wild steelhead smolts were gorged on Chinook fry. No doubt resident cutthroat and rainbow trout partake of this same feast.

Spring Chinook fry emerge January through March. Fall Chinook fry emerge February through April. Both are about 1 1/2 inches long when they become free swimming. Many Chinook salmon rear in the stream for less than one year before going to sea. Some start to out- migrate immediately upon emerging from the gravel. Most are about 1 3/4 to 2

1/4 inches long when they enter the salt. By comparison, the average out-migrating steelhead smolts are usually 5" to 7" and may be over ten inches. Chinook fry emergence is perfectly coordinated with the peak downstream migration of juvenile steelhead. Juvenile steelhead consume large amounts of Chinook fry on their way to the ocean. Chinook fry are a larger food that permit steelhead juveniles to grow quickly and compete better once they reach the ocean. Since Chinook and larger steelhead out-migrate together, this predatory relationship may continue for a while at sea. But ocean rearing Chinooks tend to feed at much greater depths than steelhead and the two populations are soon parted.

Since Chinooks out-migrate at a comparative small size, they probably don't compete much with other species for food or space while instream. They are wind-fall sustenance in the food chain department. Basin populations of every other wild salmonid specie are probably highly dependent on large healthy populations of spawning and emerging Chinooks. More Chinooks probably mean more of everything else.

Chinooks were the most abundant and most desirable salmonid for human consumption in the Columbia River basin. They were highly exploited by indigenous populations for thousands of years and have been exploited by the present civilization to the point of near extinction.

Over harvest of Chinook runs started during the U.S. Civil War. Records show that in 1877 there were over a thousand 1200' long gill nets and many fish traps in the Columbia River. All larger Columbia River tributaries also contained nets and traps. As a result, most Chinook runs were on the brink by 1875, long before any fish population surveys were made. There are no records of fish run size until the ladder counts started a Bonneville Dam in 1938. Records of harvest are sketchy. Shipping records of canned salmon are unverified since there was no government oversite. All west-slope rivers were much richer in fish runs before their Chinook populations were reduced. The catastrophic reduction in Chinook runs probably brought a biological collapse to much of the Columbia River basin, both east and west of the Cascades.

Sandy River Chinooks were some of the first heavily targeted by commercial fishermen. The mouth of the Sandy is closely proximate to the largest population area, Portland, Oregon. Nets and fish wheels probably killed most of the Sandy River Chinook runs before 1880.

A salmon hatchery was established on South Boulder Creek, a tributary to the Salmon River

(Sandy River tributary) in 1892. This hatchery was to supply Chinook eggs to bolster the failing Clackamas River runs. Chinook eggs were taken from mid-July through November from fair numbers of fish. But what hatchery people found at the mouth of South Boulder Creek in 1892 was probably no more than remnants of peak runs cropped to near extinction. Old documents record July-spawning Chinooks in both the Sandy and Clackamas drainages indicate that in the first two years of hatchery operation peak-spawning activity was in mid to late August. These upper river runs had severely declined by 1900. By 1906 the runs were so poor the hatchery was shut down because of lack of returning fish.

In 1864 the vacuum pack tinned can had been introduced to the Columbia River. Salmon meat could now be shipped long distances without fear of spoilage. Between 1864 and 1875 Chinooks were harvested so intensely that entire strongholds were completely eradicated.

Before this 11-year harvest period, the spawning and fry emergence cycles would have been months longer and much denser than they are now. The overall food chain would have been immensely richer.

Marmot Dam, built on the Sandy River in 1912, became a huge habitat and passage problem between 1912 and 1974. It impeded passage and killed downstream migrating juveniles in huge numbers. During the 1940's the Sandy River Chinook runs were on the brink of total extinction. Runs had become nearly intermittent. Some years less than fifty fish returned. Peak years brought runs numbering in the low hundreds. From 1939 until 1962 the fish ladder at Marmot Dam was closed. All anadromous fish were eliminated from the upper Sandy River basin. Fishery managers realized that an unscreened flume entrance to the Marmot diversion canal had become a death trap for a high percentage of downstream migrating fish. Fish entering the canal eventually had to escape through turbines in the Bull Run generators. Mortality was near 100 percent. Instead of forcing the power company to screen the canal entrance, fish managers opted to stop migration of anadromous fish above the dam. They trapped all the fish and took their eggs to be raised in a hatchery built below the dam. The project was a disaster. Runs further declined. They reached a low in 1943 when only 3 female Chinook showed up for egg take.

In 1951 the Marmot flume was screened to prevent entrapment of juveniles, and the fish ladder was reopened in 1962. As Chinooks started to re-enter the basin, run and spawning activity timing became critical. Few fish were available, and those reaching sexual maturity too early or too late had difficulty finding mates.

In 1974 crucial water flow management improvements on the Sandy River brought more favorable conditions for Chinook migration. The Oregon Department of Fish and Wildlife started an aggressive hatchery program using mitigation money supplied by PGE. Up to 420,000 spring Chinook juveniles were raised at the Clackamas River hatchery and planted in the Sandy River and tributaries. They were derived from the lower-Willamette stock of hatchery fish, which was mostly bread from Clackamas River fish. In the 1890's, Sandy River Chinook eggs were used to restart Clackamas River runs. Now these same genetics were being used to restart Sandy River runs, as if the genetics were on loan. These Chinooks in fact adapted to the Sandy River better than to the Clackamas.

Sandy River Chinook runs prospered and grew in numbers through the 1980's and 1990's. The run of 1992 was estimated at 9,200 fish with an escapement of 6,000 spawners. Run timing had become less critical with both earlier and later returning fish able to find mates. In 2004 all releases of Spring Chinooks were "Black Holed" in the Bull Run River. Interestingly few of these chinooks return to the river before July when the Sandy is low warm and glacial colored. This management scheme has been of marginal value as a sport fishery. It is hard to know the overall impact because Chinooks have been in a down cycle throughout the region. I suspect the nature of the species has been subverted from one who had been programed to return to headwater streams to one returning a warmer lower elevation tributary.

The study of biological science assumes that if there is a niche, some organism will fill it. After 1964, much of the Chinook habitat in the upper basin had been channelized and made useless as Chinook habitat. If this habitat had been left natural, it is reasonable to assume that Chinooks would have eventually exploited all of it. It may have been possible to again have July-spawning Chinooks in the watershed. By now the food chain would have gotten richer. Spring Chinook runs might have held their own. Do to urban sprawl and climate change it is improbable for the foreseeable future.

Fall Chinook spawn in the main stem and larger tributaries throughout the basin. The largest spawning concentration in the Sandy is from the mouth of the Bull Run River to Dabney Park. These runs are comprised of four genetically different populations of fish. First to come are the Thule Chinooks. These fish are already colored when they begin to enter the river in late August. They are done spawning by late September. Next are the later bright Chinooks. They enter the river beginning in early October and are done spawning by December. Latest to come are the winter Chinooks. They enter the river December through January and may spawn as late as February (They are now probably extinct). Dispersed through the runs are Columbia River Hatchery stray Chinooks. There has been no other hatchery intervention on Sandy River Fall Chinooks since 1977.

Recent reductions in commercial harvest have brought better returns of Sandy River fall Chinooks. However, runs are still far below basin carrying capacity. The 1995 run may have been 3,500 fish, with a basin carrying capacity estimated at 10,000 to 20,000.

Think of the biomass provided by 15,000-20,000 spawners in the upper basin, rather than 1,500-5,000 spawners . . . and another 6,500 Chinooks spawning in the lower river. The food chain in the river would be much richer. Every Chinook that spawns in the watershed is money in the bank.

To protect and anchor their eggs in the river bottom, female Chinooks dig depressions in the riverbed with their tails. These depressions are created by the tail used as a shovel and by hydraulics from its oscillations. Male Chinooks deposit milt in the bottom and trailing edge of the depression. The depression is filled, and the trailing edge is mounded over with a layer of silt free gravel. This site is called a redd.

Chinook redds are often tipped up into the current. The rear interior wall of the redd is usually composed of sand and silt that collects downstream from the digging. In a large excavation this can form a mound three feet higher than the bottom of the depression. The mound assumes a flattened or slightly cupped shape in front and fan shaped at the rear. This mound could be called a dune. Dune type redds are most prominent in rivers like the main stem Sandy, Zig Zag and Deschutes below the mouth of White River—rivers containing enough sand to build mounds that prevent redds from plugging and destroying the water flow essential to oxygenating buried eggs. A layer of course rock is deposited on the tilted upstream side of this silt mound. The gravel is chosen to create a porous stratum devoid of silt, so water passes through it easily and catches eggs and milt as they flow from spawning fish. This interior of the redd is where the fertilized eggs incubate. Over this nursery is deposited a shield consisting of larger and larger stones, a layer that also allows water to pass through with little restriction. The heavy rock keeps the redd from eroding. Water flowing through the front wall of the redd is deflected by the rear wall of silt and flows into the redd from bottom to top. This too keeps silt from collecting inside the redd and insures the complete oxygenation of the eggs. If the eggs were deposited in a depression below the level of the riverbed, they would quickly smother beneath sand.

Spawning pairs of Chinooks often join redds side by side in rows perpendicular or angular to the current flow. Between these redds are trenches filled with soft flows, a washboard contour that slows water flowing along the bottom of the river. These are favored resting areas for several species of fish including trout, steelhead, and whitefish.

The digging and shaping of Chinook redds also create gravel deposits later used by smaller fish. Since Chinooks are early fall spawners their gravel deposits are ready for other later spawning species such as steelhead, coho, and trout. Spring Chinook dunes in the Salmon River trap smaller gravel along the edge of the river. In the spring this gravel is actively sought out by spawning pairs of winter steelhead. In the lower Sandy River steelhead have been observed spawning in the leading top edge of fall Chinook dunes. The hydraulics created by the dune also keeps their eggs free from silt.

Since the Chinook redd is designed to allow

water to flow through it, there are a lot of holes between the rocks that comprise it. These holes are prime habitat for many species of insects such as mayflies, stoneflies, and caddis. Chinook spawning areas are rich in insect life. Leeches and sculpins are also very prominent in Chinook redds and are food for various sizes of larger fish.

Historic records of hatchery egg samples show that the size of returning adult Chinooks has changed very little over the years. Sandy River basin adult Chinooks average fourteen to twenty-five pounds, with some specimens up to forty pounds. The average steelhead is seven to eleven pounds, the average coho five to eight pounds. Chinooks are the largest salmonids that spawn in our watershed. Their larger size means that they can exploit larger gravel than smaller fish. Big Chinooks are powerful enough to move grapefruit size rocks around. This is a different part of the streambed than is utilized by steelhead, which prefer golf ball size gravel. Resident trout are only large enough to move marble size stones.

Chinooks spawn during the lowest flows of the season and utilize the center of the streambed. Their fry tend to stay in the middle, deeper parts of the river until they are out- migrating to the ocean. Then they often follow the edge waters of higher flow and often migrate through the edge water thickets of submerged willows. They don't compete for food or space with other species, which spawn later in the season when river flows are higher.

Steelhead, trout and coho spawn in small tributaries or along the margins of rivers. Often, they spawn in places with insufficient water when Chinooks spawn. Each specie is designed to exploit a different size of gravel and therefore has different spawning habitat requirements. Their fry are also genetically designed to exploit this environment. They usually rear close to the redd through early development. In this way the fry of different species usually remains separated through infancy and don't compete with each other.

As trout and steelhead grow larger, they require more individual space and seek deeper and deeper water. Older fish will often find holds in the middle of the river. Some of the best holding water is in the drop-off behind a series of Chinook redds. These areas are often very rich in insect life. Here there is depth for cover and soft flows which make living secure and easy. This is also a prime area for intercepting emerging Chinook fry. Trout and juvenile steelhead migrate to these areas and there is often enough food and space to support large numbers. The larger fish rigorously defend the prime spots. Smaller fish patrol the margins.

Chinooks are big strong fish that are a

challenge to catch and are good to eat. But the importance of healthy Chinook runs go beyond just being grist for the human mill. They are an indicator species for the health of entire watersheds. If Chinook Salmon were ever allowed to adapt to humans, would we still need managers to protect them from us? Interesting question, isn't it?

Chapter 30

The Rock Lady

"The best and most beautiful things in the world cannot be seen or even touched — they must be felt with the heart."

--Helen Keller

It is hard to know if you, me, any of us are seeing the whole picture. Creation says the Universe should be stable. Physics says expansion should be slowing down or reversing itself. Our most learned astronomers contend that expansion of the Universe is accelerating, driven by dark energy and dark matter which can't be seen, but the effects can be measured. Supposedly the dark stuff comprises about 94% of what is around us, which means the brightest humans see about 6%. The rest of us probably see far less...or maybe...

Her name was Sylvia, but to most people she was known as The Rock Lady. No one I ever talked to knew anything about her, where she lived, or if she had any friends. She would simply appear as from the mist along the frigid winter river, often in the complete nude, bathing, swimming, or wading or just sitting bare naked blended into the shoreline scenery. She would disappear as easily. Shy and unassuming The Rock Lady concisely engineered and artistically rendered tall slim stacks of rounded grayish river rocks into statues she called “Rock People.” Together these “Rock People” formed silent communities called “Cosmic Harmony Generators” that often contained hundreds of individuals on the wide, flat gravel bars of the Sandy River in Oxbow Park. Many time, we would pass several on our floats through the canyon. Some would last for weeks or even months before floods carried them away. I made sure that my parties never intruded on her, and though we shared the same territory for nearly twenty years, I only talked to her once.

We landed on the shore of a bar covered by such a Cosmic Harmony Generator, and I walked toward a large, downed fir tree complete with a giant root-wad deposited by an earlier winter flood. It would provide cover from my clients so I might relieve myself in privacy. I had taken off my rain jacket and wading belt, then pulled-down the long zipper in the front of my chest high waders to fully open when the Rock Lady popped up from behind the roots. We were less than twenty feet apart. She was completely nude. Her long gray hair covered one shoulder and small breast. Her body was hard and lean with only a slight sag and texture of her skin betraying her age. Her demeanor was completely aloof and not provocative without the slightest hint of sensuality or self-consciousness. In a low but totally audible voice she thanked me for not knocking over any of her Rock People. I nodded and touched my hat, then asked why she worked so hard? She replied the Cosmic Harmony protected the little fish until the willows grew. I told her I didn't understand. She simply turned her back and disengaged herself. I zipped my waders back up. Regained the other parts of my attire and decided I would pee somewhere else. When I looked up, she was gone.

On the same float through Oxbow Park several years later more pieces of the puzzle finally emerged. I had parked my boat on a braided bar along a wide bend that trailed off into deeper faster water. My clients were disembarked, their angling paraphernalia dispensed, and my instructions delivered. Spring run-off was in full bloom with smoky-colored water running inches deep through the wide adjoining willow bar. Once again nature called, and I waded through the shallow running water and into the willows. Something moved slightly upstream from the stream of urine that caught my attention, it was a tiny spotted fish. Further observation disclosed others, dozens, even hundreds of them. I was standing in a school of

Chinook fry, all holding with their tiny tails oscillating against the push of the currents or darting around in the shallow water amongst the willow stalks. Everywhere I looked there were little fish. My enthusiastic report to the clients was met with a cool WTF attitude that reminded me the take- out was just downstream around the bend.

Since then, my casual survey of submerged willow bars during spring run-off periods has convinced me they are important fish habitats rarely considered when permits for new riverfront homes are being let.

And what about The Rock Lady, a survivor of Ken Kesey's Strawberry Kool-Aid Acid tests, a messenger from the distant nature worshiping Druid past, a lonely woman disconnected from society, or mother nature herself? After many years of observation, willows rarely do well in sites picked for planting by grade schoolteachers leading student groups to understand nature. They do much better in abandoned Cosmic Harmony Generator sites that often convert into vast tracts of stable willow bar habitat to nurture tiny fish.

Made in the USA
Monee, IL
17 December 2023

9497814c-8b64-4566-93df-b4e1e02865f7R02